Designing
and Planting
a Woodland
Garden

Closely planted *Acer griseum* provide a year-round framework for the garden beyond.

Designing
and Planting
a Woodland
Garden

Plants and Combinations
that Thrive in the Shade

KEITH WILEY

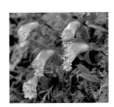

TIMBER PRESS
PORTLAND | LONDON

Photo and illustration credits appear on page 211.

The Haseltine Building   6a Lonsdale Road
133 S.W. Second Avenue, Suite 450   London NW6 6RD
Portland, Oregon 97204-3527   timberpress.co.uk
timberpress.com

Printed in China
Text design by Kate Basart/Union Pageworks
Cover design by Laken Wright

Library of Congress Cataloging-in-Publication Data

Wiley, Keith.
 Designing and planting a woodland garden: plants and combinations that thrive in the
shade/Keith
Wiley.—First edition.
    pages cm
 Other title: Plants and combinations that thrive in the shade
 Includes index.
 ISBN 978-1-60469-385-0
 1. Woodland gardening. 2. Woodland garden plants. 3. Shade-tolerant plants. I. Title. II.
Title: Plants
and combinations that thrive in the shade.
 SB439.6.W55 2014
 635.9'543—dc23
                        2014011045

A catalogue record for this book is also available from the British Library.

To my mum

Trillium grandiflorum emerges through a low carpet of the bronze-ochre young foliage of *Adiantum venustum* through which trail the purple flowers of *Phlox stolonifera*.

Camassias and candelabra primulas combine to colourful effect in early summer.

Contents

There is an otherworldly quality to ancient oak woodlands such as these, where every gnarled surface is coated and draped in moss.

Into the Woods

For nearly all my adult life, deep in the recesses of my mind, I have harboured the desire to find an established wood and make a garden there. I long ago lost count of the many woods and forests I have wandered through, dreaming of the kind of garden that I could create under their branches. I suspect that many other gardeners share this dream.

For many of us, woods and trees evoke powerful, often deeply subconscious, emotional responses. If you have a romantic inclination, you cannot fail to be moved by the moss-covered, rock-strewn gnarled oak woodlands occasionally found on the uplands of the wetter western side of the United Kingdom. Or feel as I did spiritually moved, even reverential, when dwarfed by the towering magnificence of the redwoods in northern California, the horticultural equivalent of a grand cathedral. A garden created below or among trees taps into these deep emotions to provide an uplifting and also gently protective experience that gardens without trees can never achieve.

Discovering woodlanders

When I left university I took up the post of head gardener at the Garden House in the southwest corner of England. It was a well-established garden on a cool, north-facing slope and it had many mature trees over 100 years old. Planted beneath the trees was an enviable collection of the best forms available at the time of many woodland plants. Like many garden owners on acidic soils, Lionel and Katharine Fortescue had a special fondness for trees and shrubs, especially camellias, magnolias and rhododendrons. In this damp part of the country, with its acidic soils, these woody plants thrive, but having previously gardened on alkaline soils the Fortescues also grew a wide range of perennials and some bulbs. Notable among this latter category were the erythroniums, especially the pink *Erythronium revolutum*. Multitudes of these graceful lily-like flowers emerged that first spring we were there, intermingled with drifts of blue chionodoxa and pale yellow primroses. As a relative newcomer to woodland plants, I was completely hooked.

Like many of the recently converted, my enthusiasm for this new passion knew no bounds. As I visited gardens in the United Kingdom and elsewhere, I saw more and more new woodland plants. I wanted to grow them all, but the original garden at the Garden House was already fully planted. It also became clear that the techniques we were using for growing the perennials did not suit many of the plants we were acquiring. Clearly there was no one method that was appropriate for every woodland plant and I needed to determine which conditions were needed for each to thrive. By visiting and studying plant communities in the wild, gleaning as much information as possible from experienced growers and then experimenting in an extension to the garden, bit by bit I started gaining some level of success with these woodlanders.

Eventually we moved from the Garden House to establish a nursery and garden at nearby Wildside on a south-facing field where I hoped to grow our sizeable collection of woodland plants in as natural a setting as possible. But there was not a tiny piece of shade to be had. With no time to wait for trees to grow to a perfect high canopy, I had to create shade as fast as possible. In order to create a woodland garden where there was formerly an open field, I

Woodland favourites, erythroniums rise above a carpet of moss with *Corydalis flexuosa* in the foreground.

used a number of techniques which I believe can be implemented by gardeners elsewhere, including those with much smaller plots and even tiny spaces.

Similarly, my hope in writing this book is that it opens up avenues of thinking about shade and woodland gardening which you may not have considered before. Books can only offer guidelines and this one is based on my experiences of growing woodlanders for over forty years, and how I might like to grow them in the future.

The nature of woodlands

The mention of "woodland" may conjure up romantic images of mature beeches or oaks carpeted below by swathes of bluebells (in northwestern Europe) and trilliums or other wildflowers (in North America). Ancient woodlands or old-growth forests with venerable trees, wherever they occur in the world, represent the traditional vision of deeply shaded woodland. But in fact these ancient forests are relatively scarce, and woodlands come in many different shades.

In the United Kingdom, familiar wooded landscapes include coppiced woods, where the trees are cut to the ground on perhaps a fifteen-year cycle, and forestry plantations (both coniferous and deciduous). In North America, the tremendous diversity of forested land includes the eastern deciduous forest, the coniferous forests of the Pacific Northwest, the high-elevation aspens of the southern Rockies, and the pine woods found in the Northeast and through the southern states as far as Florida, among others. But these densely forested areas are not the only woodland habitats. There are also less obvious opportunities for creating woodland conditions, such as fruit orchards, loose aggregations of small trees on the moors or mountainsides and marginal land partly colonized by shrubby trees like hawthorns (*Crataegus laevigata*) in the United Kingdom, for instance, or by scrubby pinyon in the Sierra Nevadas.

The UK Forestry Commission defines a woodland as "land under stands of trees with a canopy cover of at least 20 percent (or having the potential to achieve this), including integral open space, and including felled areas that are awaiting restocking". Interestingly, "there is no minimum height for trees to form a woodland at maturity, so the definition includes woodland scrub." There is also no minimum size for a woodland, so areas down to as little as a quarter of an acre (0.1 hectares) are included in the UK statistics. Elsewhere in the world, the definition of a woodland varies from a canopy cover of 10 to 50 percent and a minimum height at maturity up to 16 ft. (5 m).

In the Pacific Northwest, a Garry oak woodland has an intangible quality of age, similar to ancient apple orchards in the United Kingdom.

Any gardener with an interest in nature should take a pilgrimage to the redwood forests of California and experience the cathedral-like atmosphere imparted by these towering giants.

In a woodland in northern Spain, the autumnal trees are starting to reveal a picture-postcard tracery of trunks and branches.

In many of these technical definitions, there is actually a very small percentage of shaded area. Clearly in many woods there are significant areas open to the sky.

How can such technical definitions affect how we think about woodland gardens? Well, acknowledging that woodlands are diverse and complicated is a first step towards broadening our attitudes about what can be considered a woodland garden. Observing plants in their native habitats may also challenge established wisdom about what could thrive in a garden setting. Many of the shrubs, perennials and bulbs commonly classified as "woodlanders" or "shade plants" come from a range of different habitats, from deepest shade to open hillside. Even many of the classic woodland plants grow in forest clearings where they may be in full sun for many hours at a stretch and, indeed, these glades may be where the greatest range of plant species is found in native woodlands. For this book, I define a woodlander as any plant that will grow and (if relevant) flower happily in a semi-shady site without looking incongruous.

Woodlanders and shade

Given how many different habitats forest plants have colonized in the wild and how many species are dependent on very specific habitats—from shady, moisture-retentive ravines at one end of the spectrum to sun-baked dunes at the other—it's no surprise that there is a vast number of plants sold as shade lovers, without much more information about their cultivation needs. Many of the most special woodland plants become available to gardeners due to the efforts of intrepid plant collectors. These treasures make their way into nurseries and are purchased by gardeners at some cost. But when planted in the limited conditions our gardens offer, we wonder why these expensive specimens are not thriving. It speaks volumes for the resilience of plants that so many manage to perform tolerably well despite less-than-perfect growing conditions.

In order to grow many woodlanders successfully, you may need to create conditions in the garden that more closely represent those in the plant's native habitat. For instance, many traditional woodland plants grow in the wild at high altitudes where there is little tree cover but the atmosphere is cool, the rainfall and humidity significantly high and the air frequently misty. Even in these conditions, plants such as moisture-loving primulas growing in permanently damp soil may flag if exposed to direct afternoon sun. If you transfer these plants down to lower altitudes into a garden where conditions are drier and hotter in summer, the only way to keep them happy

Arisaema are plants of the woodland floor, so even though this *A. consanguineum* growing out of a rock in its native Yunnan is an extremely rare sight, understanding why it can thrive there can help us understand the conditions it needs to do well in a home garden.

is by providing them with some shade. Fortunately, there are many ways to accomplish this.

A host of factors affect how much shade is needed by a particular plant in a particular garden, including annual rainfall and its distribution through the year, summer temperatures, soil moisture levels, latitude, altitude, which direction the garden faces and susceptibility to wind, to name a few. Your soil's pH and drainage also influence the range of plants that can be grown.

Woodland garden style

In the early 20th century a woodland garden style was established by wealthy landowners, who were generally in possession of large estates. Many of these still exist today, and they are gardens on a grand scale, where mature trees are underplanted with shrubs, mainly with the azaleas, magnolias and rhododendrons that flooded into cultivation at that time. Often the primary planting consideration seems to have been whether there was another square yard into which an azalea or rhododendron could be squeezed, regardless of whether the colour clashes with its neighbours. The results at flowering time can be jaw dropping.

Sited in sheltered valleys on acidic soils, many of these understorey shrubs become arboreal due to the perfect growing conditions. Visiting a garden like Mount Usher, near Dublin in Ireland, it is hard to think of some of these huge imposing specimens as shrubs. In this style of garden, spring bulbs are grown on a similarly large scale, with huge drifts of just one or two species. I was brought up to revere the splendour of these majestic gardens. At one time they exemplified to me what a woodland garden was meant to be.

But, spectacular as they were during the spring-flowering extravaganza, there was little need in these gardens to prolong the flowering period into the summer by incorporating perennials. Once the spring display had ended, many landowners left their estates for the season. In those rare gardens where perennials were planted, the trend was to place them in herbaceous borders or in a cutting garden away from the woodland. It wasn't until towards the last third of the century that pressure to extend the flowering season (perhaps to attract garden visitors) took hold and more summer-flowering perennials came to be incorporated into planting schemes. This coincided with a fundamental shift, when people with considerably smaller properties developed an interest in gardening and garden plants. Planting schemes in these gardens were limited by the seasons, and their owners took little notice of any particular plant's natural habitat other than for general factors such as the amount of sun, or moist versus well-drained sites. To my eye, this led to many incongruous plant combinations and left many beautiful but less flamboyant woodland perennials languishing in semi-obscurity.

The new woodland garden

As so often in my gardening life it was by observing plants in the wild, particularly the seemingly effortless way they combine, that sparked my desire to experiment with a wider range of woodland plants. My general approach to gardening tends to be holistic, which means that I see the whole woodland garden environment as a single unit which is in balance from the tallest tree down to the smallest bulb. Gardens like this do not rely solely on a blaze of spring glory but instead have a natural look that is always changing. This differs structurally from the stereotypical woodland garden by having fewer and less densely planted shrubs in the understorey layer, which in turn lets more light reach the woodland floor and allows a wider range of plants to grow there.

In a natural woodland garden, the overall shape, structure and colours of the garden should be in harmony throughout the year, and perennials, bulbs

Large-scale plantings of rhododendrons and azaleas under mature trees at the Winterthur garden in Delaware were common where acid soils allowed their cultivation.

Candelabra primulas, rodgersias and other moisture-loving perennials crowd the lower, damper sections of a glade at Wildside.

In their preferred growing conditions, perennials can form naturalistic combinations, such as here when *Corydalis flexuosa* self-seeded into the fern *Adiantum aleuticum* 'Japonicum'. *Impatiens omeiana* is the third member of the grouping.

This combination of witch hazel and *Chionochloa rubra* is a good basis for a winter-themed garden. To extend the flowering season fill the gaps between the grasses with spring- and summer-blooming bulbs and woodland perennials.

In winter, the bare branches of trees and shrubs collect drops of water to create shimmering strings of jewel-like garlands. Maintaining the natural shape of the plant keeps the overall effect balanced.

and grasses all have their moment in the spotlight. In fact, a well-designed woodland garden is very much a year-round garden. In winter, the shape of the trees, both canopy and understorey, are reason enough for celebration, but given a coating of snow or hoar frost they are turned into a romantic dreamland. Colourful trunks and twigs just add to the seasonal appeal, with an occasional evergreen shrub providing contrast.

In spring, the real glory of the blooming woodland garden happens. Various levels of the woody canopy create unique vertical colour combinations that reach a zenith when the burgeoning leaves of the trees display a shimmering array of verdant freshness. The woodland garden in spring exudes exuberance that imbues birds and humans alike with a glorious joie de vivre.

After such heady heights, the summer garden almost *needs* a period of reflective calm, and here too the woodland garden does not disappoint. There are still plenty of plants that will flower right through to the first frosts but an air of general bloated contentedness descends upon the wood, its welcoming shade providing succour from the summer heat. Finally the autumn foliage appears for a few tantalizingly unpredictable weeks when the whole garden is supercharged with glorious colour. As this crescendo finally dims and the leaves on the trees and shrubs drop, the perennials and grasses pick up the rhythm in more muted hushed tones of ochres and browns as they start to close down operations for the season before gradually fading into silence whereupon the whole cycle begins again.

Understanding your site

There seems to be a commonly held view that shady conditions are a bit of a problem for the gardener. Although it is true they do throw up certain challenges, they are challenges to be relished, so long as you try to develop an understanding of the underlying constraints these conditions impose. As we have seen, there is no single set of conditions that covers all the variety implied by the term "woodland", and it is only by analyzing your individual garden that you can devise suitable planting schemes for it. The fact that woodlands vary so much in the wild with a correspondingly large range of plants suited to this diversity suggests there are solutions for every home garden.

Clearly, where you live will influence how you develop your woodland garden. Even in the United Kingdom—which has a very narrow range of generally advantageous growing conditions for temperate woodlanders— there are significant differences in site conditions, including the type of tree cover, light intensity and duration, soil type, structure and depth, moisture levels, site aspect, shelter from wind and root infestation. In the cooler, wetter west of England where I live, the moisture-retentive loam means that many woodland plants recommended for at least partial shade will grow perfectly happily in full sun. In drier areas with higher summer temperatures or more quick-draining sandy soils, some shade will almost certainly be needed, the amount depending on the moisture retentiveness of your soil, or how much you are prepared to irrigate the area.

Making few basic assessments of your site will help you to avoid such pitfalls as overambitious expectations, and will go a long way to avoiding disappointments, unnecessary expense and backache. It is all too easy to imagine a steep wooded ravine as a home from home for Himalayan rhododendrons which generally need shelter from the wind, without taking into account the back-breaking work involved in thinning the tree canopy to obtain optimum light conditions for these shrubs, or removing huge root systems to accommodate them (as a friend of immense plant knowledge soon discovered when he attempted it).

Sunlight and shadows penetrate through the branches of magnolias to create patterns of light on the beautiful woodlander *Trillium albidum*.

How shady is your site?

The first thing to consider in your garden is the density of any existing tree cover and any understorey plants. In general terms, the higher the canopy the better. Because the vast majority of woodland plants, including their seedlings, make nearly all their growth in the spring period this is when maximum light is required. For instance, *Erythronium* seeds (excluding the montane species) germinate in early spring and have completed their annual above-ground life cycle by midspring before the leaf canopy closes over. With most deciduous trees, including magnolias, this usually happens in late spring. If you have coniferous trees—or deciduous trees with large leaves that leaf out very early, such as horse chestnut—you will have to significantly prune up the branches to lessen the deep shade they cast.

The light beneath the deciduous canopy is constantly changing, not just through different seasons of the year but also through the hours of each day. As summer approaches, established woodland plants appreciate the shade afforded by the leaf cover of the canopy, but they still need good light levels and generally will flower much better with some direct light every day. This has to be balanced with protection from direct midday sun, which can

Deciduous trees which leaf out in early spring or have large leaves

- *Acer platanoides* Norway maple
- *Acer pseudoplatanus* sycamore
- *Aesculus* horse chestnut, buckeye
- *Carpinus betulus* hornbeam
- *Castanea* sweet chestnut
- *Magnolia × soulangeana* and other types with leaves of similar size or larger
- *Platanus* plane tree
- *Quercus rubra* red oak
- *Sorbus aria* whitebeam

Deciduous trees which leaf out in late spring

- *Acer griseum* paperbark maple
- *Acer palmatum* Japanese maple
- *Carya* hickory
- *Cercis canadensis* Eastern redbud
- *Cladrastis* yellowwood
- *Cornus* dogwood
- *Fagus sylvatica* beech
- *Fraxinus* ash (aggressive surface roots)
- *Juglans* walnut
- *Koelreuteria paniculata* goldenrain tree, pride of India
- *Liriodendron* tulip tree
- *Magnolia* (surface rooting)
- *Quercus* oak
- *Robinia pseudoacacia* black locust
- *Tilia* lime

Trees which cast lighter shade

- *Acer griseum* paperbark maple
- *Acer japonicum, A. palmatum* Japanese maple
- *Amelanchier* redbud
- *Betula* birch
- *Cercidiphyllum japonicum* katsura tree
- *Cercis canadensis* redbud
- *Cornus* dogwood
- *Eucalyptus* (evergreen)
- *Ginkgo biloba* ginkgo
- *Gleditsia* honey locust
- *Gymnocladus dioica* Kentucky coffeetree
- *Koelreuteria paniculata* goldenrain tree, pride of India
- *Larix decidua* larch
- *Liquidambar styraciflua* sweetgum
- *Olea europaea* olive (evergreen)
- *Quercus* oak
- *Robinia pseudoacacia* black locust, false acacia
- *Sophora japonica* Japanese pagoda tree
- *Sorbus* mountain ash, rowan, whitebeam

scorch the foliage of many woodlanders. Similarly in winter if shoots or flowers have frozen overnight, the early morning sun shining directly onto them can cause considerable damage.

Dappled light and shafts of sunlight emphasize light and shade, and as any photographer will tell you, provide depth and contrast to pictures in a way the glaring light of full sun cannot approach. These subtleties of light are matched by the understated charm of many woodland flowers, which often eschew flamboyance for more intricate detail and graceful form. Even those woodland plants renowned for seasonal extravagance of outrageous flowering such as azaleas and rhododendrons, are toned down in this arboreal setting by the massed greenery of the canopy itself.

Clearly the key factor in any woodland garden, whether established or new, is to find the right balance of sunlight to shade. Trying to approximate the shade you have to that found in a native woodland is a good start, as it can suggest the relative density and diversity of the flora at ground level. Many coniferous woods have thin vegetation levels below them unless the trees are widely spaced. Walk through such a forest and the reasons become obvious—the environment is dark, dry and nutrient poor from the excessive needle drop. In an ideal woodand situation, sunlight should reach the ground in most of the site for two to three hours per day, preferably more in the spring. Clearly deciduous tree cover gives more planting options than evergreens. Good choices will cast light shade or hold their branches very high allowing light to penetrate, such as oaks.

The understorey

In many natural woods there is an understorey of smaller trees and shrubs below the high level canopy of trees. You can recreate this understorey in a home garden, preferably with small flowering trees or evergreens that provide textural diversity, shelter, mystery and privacy.

This woody understorey of shrubs, smaller trees and climbers brings a set of slightly different challenges than the higher tree canopy. On the negative side, the thickness of the understorey in native copses and woods can squeeze out lower-growing flowering plants. In the United Kingdom, introduced species such as *Rhododendron ponticum* and natives like brambles, ivy and old man's beard (*Clematis viticella*) completely choke many woods, denying any chance for smaller-growing plants. In the United States, the culprits may be wild honeysuckle or Japanese knotweed, or even garden escapees like holly or Russian vine (*Polygonum baldschuanicum*). Every country I have visited seems to have its own set of woodland thugs, unfortunately often introduced species, which have to be completely removed as almost nothing can compete with such aggressive spreaders.

On the positive side, a balanced, controlled understorey can provide shelter, scents, coloured foliage and flowers throughout the year, vastly extending the interest of the woodland from spring-flowering ephemerals. It is a balancing act that will repay careful thought and reward those who succeed with unbridled pleasure.

In a smaller setting, if your garden has no large trees, these understorey woody plants can function as the primary source of shade and shelter for any lower-growing perennials and bulbs. This is exactly what I have done at Wildside where there were originally no trees at all, although I did add some fast-growing birch trees to provide high shading and double as "nurse trees" for the understorey plants. The natural habitat of understorey trees, shrubs and climbers is typically in part shade, but they are often equally at home in full sun in northern temperate climates and may actually flower better as a result of the higher light intensities.

The structure of your soil

Another fundamental consideration in a woodland garden is the structure of the soil. Ideal soil conditions are found in a deciduous wood of widely spaced, deep-rooting trees with a high canopy and very little woody understorey to stop the light reaching the ground in spring. These soils are often deeply enriched with leafmould which makes them open, friable and free draining. It is no surprise that where these conditions exist, for example in

Trillium grandiflorum carpet a wood in Michigan, where the humus-rich soil enables them to thrive and spread into vast colonies.

From left to right, *Rhododendron glaucophyllum* 'Prostratum', variegated *Pieris japonica* 'Little Heath' and *Daphne* 'Eternal Fragrance' form a compact understorey group providing shelter and some shade to smaller bulbs and perennials. *Daphne* ×*burkwoodii* 'Albert Burkwood' and Japanese maples frame the background.

parts of Maryland and Virginia, the woodland flora of spring ephemerals including bloodroot, mertensias and trilliums are a wonder to behold and a cause of serious gardener envy.

So do you have the loose, open friable soil of ideal woodland conditions or something more closely resembling dusty concrete? If you have a woodland area where perennials or herbaceous weeds are already growing, and you can drive a fork into the ground and lift up some soil without damaging either the fork or some part of your anatomy, then you are in luck. In most gardens there are probably a few obstacles to be negotiated first. If the soil is riddled with shallow tree roots, it can make planting at best difficult and at worst impossible. For example ash, horse chestnut, sycamore, most evergreen trees (especially conifers) and to a lesser extent beech trees have very dense, aggressive root systems likely to infiltrate any new territory. Many conifers also have shallow roots. On the other hand, trees like oaks generally send their roots deeper and are the perfect shade trees.

Creating space for woodlanders under trees isn't restricted of course to native trees. Try the fork test under an established magnolia for example and it is doubtful you will even get the fork into the ground in the first place. Whether native or exotic, shade trees with dense impenetrable root masses like this are inevitably going to limit your choices.

Common trees with shallow or dense roots

- *Acer platanoides* Norway maple
- *Acer pseudoplatanus* sycamore
- *Aesculus hippocastanum* horse chestnut
- *Betula* birch
- *Cornus* dogwood
- *Fagus* beech
- *Fraxinus* ash
- *Magnolia*
- *Platanus occidentalis* plane tree
- *Populus nigra* poplar
- *Salix* willow

Erythronium citrinum has colonized the ground beneath manzanita bushes (*Arctostaphylos*) on a hillside in southern Oregon. Together with the cream flowers and pinkish trunks of the manzanita, this created a wonderfully harmonious combination.

Repetition of grasses and shapes, and the careful placements of taller specimens and bold foliage plants imbue this section of Mary Gore's garden with a restful, sophisticated woodland atmosphere.

The Woodlanders

Whether large or small, the key composition in the woodland garden is one of layers. Regardless of plant type, whether it be a small tree, shrub, perennial, bulb, grass, alpine or fern, if it possesses a graceful, elegant habit I prefer to grow it in a position where it is surrounded by lower-growing plants so that its form can be best appreciated. Thus, shape, habit and placement are all worthy consideration as you begin to plant your woodland.

Bulbs, the woodland ephemerals

One of the joys of visiting any garden, even famous ones like Chanticleer, is to observe how other gardeners interpret spaces. Lovely as these camassias are in isolation, I would want to try candelabra primulas in place of the grassy stream edges to extend the flowering season.

Over the years I have experimented with growing bulbs in a range of different positions within the garden but have come to the conclusion that it is better to keep them in the same general areas for aesthetic and pragmatic reasons. I now congregate many of the smaller plants, including the more diminutive spring bulbs in relatively limited areas of garden. This has numerous advantages. First, all the plants are of similar size so there are fewer problems with having to rescue some small special plant from the clutches of a taller neighbour. Being small, their flowers and foliage are all of a similar scale and therefore likely to blend together better. It also concentrates the almost relentless weeding efforts into a relatively confined space. If many of the spring bulbs and other ephemerals are planted together, when

they have all died down, there is an easy opportunity to make sure the bed is clear of all weeds and a chance to mulch it.

Part of the reason I prefer to grow ephemerals away from most perennials is because I have found unless you are constantly vigilant, years of patiently waiting for your bulbs to spread can be wasted in a single season if the bulbs are allowed to be badly overgrown by taller plants when the bulbs are still in full growth. The seedlings of neighbouring perennials such as aquilegias or *Campanula lactiflora* can grow and bulk up with such alarming speed that nearby small bulbs and perennials are lost unless you can keep the aggressive interlopers in check. So although I make exceptions in particular circumstances with snowdrops and wood anemones, I tend to limit mixed plantings of bulbs and taller perennials to the taller bulbs like lilies and camassias, or bold-foliaged tuberous plants like arisaemas, roscoeas and trilliums. On a smaller scale this is still true even when using low-spreading perennials such as dicentras.

I am a firm believer anyway in the principle of placing together plants that flower at the same time of year to make a glorious spectacle of them, rather than diluting their effect by spreading them all over the garden. It is a principle I have employed for many years in nearly all the plantings I make—I call it the "bluebell wood" effect. A single bluebell is nothing special, but a wood of them is magical. It applies across the board. A single trillium *is* actually exciting but is not in the same league as a mass of them. In

Erythronium 'White Beauty' is surrounded here by self-seeded *Corydalis shimienensis.* The corydalis is dense enough to provide quite efficient ground cover but not so dense as to prevent the erythronium from growing through it.

relation to woodland plants (and specifically bulbs) this becomes most relevant with spring bulbs.

When I came to the Garden House there was a small area around the base of an old copper beech where woodland bulbs had naturalized. The season started with *Galanthus* 'Atkinsii', moved on through *Chionodoxa sardensis* to *Erythronium revolutum*, then *Cyclamen repandum* and *Scilla campanulatus*, then finishing up with *Camassia leichtlinii*. Four months of colour from a bed no bigger than a double garage.

Sunlight streaming through the leaves of beech trees adds to the magic of the sights and smells of a bluebell wood in late spring in Wiltshire, England.

In an open glade of maples at the Garden House in Devon, *Crocus tommasinianus* and *C.* 'Vanguard' combine to gradually build a naturalistic effect. Only the species *C. tomasinianus* will self-seed, although hybrids between them will appear.

I first tried this on a larger scale with a bulb meadow at the Garden House, on a north-facing slope surrounded by large magnolias, with a scattering of mature conifers and evergreen photinias and pieris. This was fabulous at flowering time in its own right with the mass of white magnolia flowers set off against the dark conifers and the bronze and red of the young leaves of the bushes. These trees and shrubs were quite widely spaced, giving a woodland glade effect with the open centre further punctuated by shade-giving mature deciduous azaleas which have heavenly scented flowers in late spring. I thought that I could make it even more special by carpeting the ground beneath and between these trees with a whole series of spring woodland plants, starting with snowdrops and *Cyclamen coum*, running through the main spring flush with chionodoxas, dwarf daffodils, erythroniums, primroses, scillas and wood anemones, right through to the late summer- and autumn-flowering cyclamen, colchicums and autumn crocus. It worked spectacularly well, with over 200 different taxa blended into tapestries of ever-changing colour and texture hugging the contours of the ground and flowering for five or six months each year. I regret that the demands of the garden at that time of year meant I never took a photograph that did it justice when it was at its glorious best.

Woodland perennials

Perennials form the core of many woodland plantings, and although I love their flowers what is more important for me is the overall shape and habit of the plants and the colours and textures of the foliage. This is especially necessary in the woodland garden, where flowers generally are more subdued than their sun-basking counterparts. In addition, many shade-loving woodlanders come from parts of the world where heavy rains can be expected at their flowering time and so have evolved downward-facing flowers to protect their precious pollen and stigmas. Their subtlety and coyness adds to their charm but it is their foliage and shape that we spend the greater part of the year with.

Among the perennial choices for woodland plants are some basic plant shapes that you should consider repeating time and again and which in combination bestow an authentic natural feel to any shade planting. By surrounding individuals or small groups of plants which have a strong distinct shape of their own with a carpet of lower-growing plants, you are able to emphasize the distinctive shape of the taller specimens. The phrase "the whole is greater than the sum of its parts" seems to apply in this case, but each group is worth considering in turn.

Perennial growth habits

Group 1 Upright, then arching

These include species of *Disporum*, *Polygonatum*, and *Maianthemum* (formerly *Smilacina*). Smaller, but similary shaped plants include *Streptopus simplex*, *Tricyrtis* and *Uvularia*, as well as the beautiful maidenhair fern (*Adiantum pedatum*). All have good foliage and a strong architectural shape which to me is the classic woodlander habit. The spear-like shoots emerge in spring and usually grow rapidly skywards before arching or branching, a practice which has presumably evolved to take the stems clear of surrounding competition before investing in the serious business of flower and seed production. Place plants with this type of growth habit where they can rise above lower-growing plants, as you would lose much of the drama by crowding them into a bed with similar-sized plants. Other plants with this habit often have flowers frequently suspended below the arching stems, but their foliage and overall impression is similar if less extravagant.

Heuchera 'Southern Comfort' is planted here in a small grouping, set against a ground-hugging covering of flowering thyme.

Shortia uniflora is a valuable sub-shrub that merits a special spot in the woodland garden, where it will slowly form a compact mound of rounded glossy evergreen leaves.

Group 2 Low, clump forming

This large group of plants forms the basis of perennial planting in woodland conditions, and includes *Corydalis*, *Epimedium*, *Helleborus*, *Heuchera*, *Omphalodes*, *Pulmonaria*, *Pachyphragma* and the fern *Adiantum aleuticum* 'Subpumilum'. They grow 8–24 in. (20–60 cm) high and wide, forming compact clumps that I prefer to place in small scattered groups of no more than three or four individuals. To plant a larger area with a single species I place them in groups in such a way that from certain angles they appear to be continuous. Hellebores are a case in point. Planting them en masse in a solid block means losing the individual plant's grace and charm.

Group 3 Tightly clumping, mainly evergreen

I include in this group *Clintonia*, *Galax*, *Haberlea*, *Ourisia*, *Pteridophyllum*, *Ramonda*, *Saxifraga*, *Shortia*, *Soldanella*, *Ophiopogon* and *Liriope*. Many reach only about 6 in. (15 cm) in height and spread very slowly. Some, such as *Pteridophyllum* and *Shortia*, are treasures best grown with other special woodland plants in beds solely designated for them. If planted in the garden, ramondas are safest planted where they do not have close competition. The others can be grown in very small groups among lower spring bulbs and other ephemerals such as *Dicentra cucullaria* or *Anemone nemorosa*, as their evergreen nature comes in useful when their neighbours have retreated back below ground. The liriope and ophiopogon offer a textural foil of grass-like foliage to these low plantings. All the rest of this group is shown to best advantage if grown on a near-vertical bank, such as peat block walls or shaded retaining dry stone walls. Leave large gaps between the stones and backfill with a "woodsy" soil mixture.

Group 4 Prostrate, tight to the ground

These are plants that form low mats of foliage such as *Ajuga*, *Chrysoplenium*, *Lysimachia nummularia* 'Aurea', *Phlox stolonifera* and *P. procumbens*, *Pratia pedunculata*, *Saxifraga stolonifera* and *S. cuscutiformis*, *Soleirolia*, *Vinca minor* and *Viola cornuta*. With the exception of the phlox and the viola, this group is too vigorous to plant alongside any clump-forming plant that grows less than 1 ft. (30 cm) high, but they can form a carpet around those from Group 2, emphasizing the distinct shapes of the taller plants. If the carpet created by the plants in this group is less than 1 in. (2 cm) deep (which is the case even with the rampageous thug that is *Pratia pedunculata*), you can still grow many bulbs and other ephemerals up through it; I have successfully grown erythroniums, roscoeas and *Corydalis shimienensis* through carpeting plants in this group.

Group 5 Low, spreading

These plants grow up to 12–18 in. (30–45 cm) high, spreading underground to form sizeable patches, including *Cardamine*, *Corydalis flexuosa*, *Dicentra*, *Geranium macrorhizum* and *G. oxonianum*, *Ranunculus* and *Viola*, the older established epimediums like *Epimedium perralderianum* and, among the ferns, *Adiantum venustum* and *Gymnocarpium dryopteris*. I treat them as a separate group because of their vigour. They will happily

associate with Group 1 and the more vigorous members of Groups 2 and 4, as well as taller plants. Where large blocks of ground-covering plants are wanted, this is the group to use. I remember once visiting a young garden of four or five acres in Kent that managed to create the impression of an established wood with massed plantings of mainly *Geranium macrorhizum* and *G. ×oxonianum* under thinned plantation plantings of young pines and massed heathers. Maybe it was rather "samey" but it was also an object lesson in what could be achieved in a very short time requiring minimum maintenance.

Deep purple 'Huntercombe Purple', mauve 'Maggie Mott' and yellow 'Moonlight' violas merge with *Geranium asphodeloides* at the front of a shady border.

Group 6 Bold foliage plants

These include *Diphyllea cymosa*, *Hosta*, *Ligularia*, *Podophyllum*, *Rodgersia* and *Veratrum* as well as some of the disporums and maianthemums. With finely divided but equally bold foliage are many of the ferns, especially *Blechnum tabulare*, *Dryopteris crassirhizoma*, *D. wallichiana*, *Osmunda*, *Polystichum munitum*, *Woodwardia radicans* and of course the unrivalled tree ferns (*Dicksonia* and *Cyathea*) if you are lucky enough to have a frost-free garden in which to grow them. Rather than lone specimens of these striking plants, I prefer small clumps and drifts of a single variety, interplanted with similar-sized groups of different-textured foliage. The bigger lilies and particularly the magnificent cardiocrinum would look especially good in this sort of company. Even for small gardens there are many plants from this group, including ferns, hellebores, hostas, podophyllums, pulmonarias and roscoeas. In a compact space, scale down the plant size and look for slightly smaller leaf size.

Group 7 Tall, clump forming

Among the taller plants, I grow *Actaea*, *Aconitum*, *Aster cordifolius*, *Campanula*, *Patrinia scabiosifolia* and *Thalictrum* in full sun, but these will all also do well in partial shade. They certainly don't look out of place in a woodland setting although in too much shade they can become "drawn up" and then flop over. Staking plants seems to me out of place in a natural woodland garden, so I place these towards the back of plantings. Other tall plants can remain upright with no assistance, such as *Aconitum carmichaelii* 'Kelmscott', which flowers in early autumn with hooded flowers of a lovely shade of lavender-blue. Its habit makes it a good counterpoint to *Aster cordifolius*, one of the few Michaelmas daisies that will grow happily in partial shade. *Aster* 'Little Carlow', a hybrid of *A. cordifolius*, grows best in full sun but because of its ancestry is also worth trying in partial shade.

Group 8 Grasses and grass-like plants

In a shady or semi-shady situation, the dreamy waving flowerheads of grasses serving as a major counterfoil to masses of blooming perennials is best forgotten. Instead, think of grasses mainly as foliage plants that can provide variation of texture and form. There are some grasses that will flower in semi-shady conditions, but they are generally more muted than their sun-loving counterparts. There are also perennials and small shrubs with distinctly narrow straplike foliage which resemble grasses, such as *Astelia*, *Iris*, *Liriope*, *Ophiopogon* and *Schizostylis*.

As suggested by its common name of umbrella leaf, *Diphyllea cymosa* has dramatic and handsome leaves that can show good colour in fall.

Aster 'Little Carlow' is one of the finest of all Michaelmas daisies and provides a striking tall specimen in a semi-shaded spot.

Iris foliage can lend the structural effect of grasses to plant combinations, such as this patch of *Iris innominata* seedlings with the European native wood melick, *Melica uniflora*.

Foliage colour

Coloured foliage is important in any garden, woodland or otherwise. I prefer to limit variegated plants, and those with bold colours and forms, to areas of the garden near human-made structures such as the house, other buildings, or walls and pergolas. Here, in conjunction with containers or other garden ornamentation, the plants can act as focal points and bring uplifting colour and vibrancy to the garden. In these contexts the way the plant is set off by the backdrop is almost as important as the plant itself. For example, when surrounded by dark-coloured soil, most purple-leaved plants such as some ajugas become close to invisible, or appear almost dead, as in the case of the sedge *Carex comans*. However, when these plants are set against a mulch of golden gravel their colour suddenly "sings".

If your aim is to create a naturalistic garden that blends with the surrounding landscape then variegation, especially strong variegation, and gold- and purple-leaved plants should be treated with circumspection. These colours, if soft and suffused with green, would enhance any landscape but in strong hues tend to stand out rather incongruously. Greys and silvers on the other hand are more companionable, especially in hotter, sunnier climates.

The silver variegation of *Athyrium nipponicum* 'Pictum' and *Saxifraga stolonifera* has been skilfully used here to accentuate the lichen growth and to contrast with the form and texture of the boulder over which they grow.

In a semi-shady spot with a dark background the yellow-greens of these foliage plants stand out. Silver variegation is restricted to a secondary, lower-level role in the forms of athyriums and brunneras.

Woodland treasures

The more interested you become in plants, the more you realize there are almost limitless tempting choices, but certain very desirable small plants are not easy to grow in the open garden amid more robust and amenable plants. Any selection of such woodland treasures might include an eclectic mix of small shrubs, orchids, bulbs and perennials such as hepaticas or choice primulas. Dedicated, passionate gardeners with smaller plots can grow these aristocrats (and larger gardens with a correspondingly large number of staff can also manage it). However, after trying for years to incorporate these toys, treasures and specials of the woodland world into relatively large gardens, I have reluctantly acknowledged that it is generally beyond my abilities.

I have listed some of my favourite treasures in the plant directory, although I have tried to limit those rarities that are difficult to obtain. I urge you to try growing some of them because successful cultivation is disproportionately rewarding. However, I recommend you grow them in specific areas where you can manipulate the soil conditions and where good air movement, light and freedom from taller neighbours can be guaranteed. Many gardeners understand this and grow their treasures in dedicated rockeries and alpine beds; some prefer to keep their most special alpines and other plants confined to even more pampered existences in climate-controlled alpine houses.

In the open garden, raised beds are really the best place to grow desirable but difficult woodland treasures, and they offer the advantage of bringing the plants closer to view. You can modify the soil structure mainly by the addition of grit, sand and leafmould (and with peat if your conscience allows) to create a soil mixture that is moisture retentive yet very free draining. The superlative peat beds of the Gothenburg Botanical Garden in Sweden are made up of about 50 percent mineral content (a blend of coarse sand and grit), 25 percent peat and 25 percent organic matter (leafmould by choice) in raised beds behind supporting banks of large peat blocks. In my own raised beds, I incorporate a layer of well-rotted farmyard manure below the immediate rooting area of any new plants. Other gardeners find wood ash beneficial at similar depths, but each plantsperson will have their own recipe for success. The reward (and there is plenty) is the pleasure of basking in the beauty these little gems have to offer when growing well. Later you can always move surplus plants out into the garden proper.

There is really nothing better than large Swedish peat blocks for the retaining walls of these beds, because of their natural appearance and wonderful water retention, but the use of peat is of course controversial. I have also built raised beds with natural stone, sawn tanalised wood, railway sleepers and concrete blocks and all have worked perfectly well.

I grow special plants like these *Erythronium* hybrids in "intensive care units" to provide them with ideal conditions to grow well and so that I can easily compare between varieties.

This snaking path at Wildside, sunken between raised banks, has been planted with scented deciduous azaleas and Japanese maples which provide tiered layers of shade. In late spring woodland perennials and ferns flourish, while earlier in the season snowdrops, erythroniums and wood anemones thrive on these banks under the then leafless deciduous canopy.

Creating a Woodland Garden

Whether you have the bones of a woodland garden on your property or are starting as I did at Wildside with no shade at all, there are steps you can take to ensure success for your woodland plantings. Remember that your goal is to create an environment where your chosen plants can thrive. To a large extent this will depend on your local climatic and soil conditions. If you live in an area with high summer temperatures and strong sunlight, shade will be your priority. In areas with little rainfall and dry soils you may need to provide extra moisture. If your garden is like mine, with a year-round wet climate or in wet soils, drainage will be the key.

Preparing an existing woodland

There are essentially two major challenges when you are starting to build a garden where there are already established mature trees. One is getting sufficient light to reach the ground and the second is the composition of the soil where your plants will be growing, especially the degree of tree root infestation. There are steps you can take to ameliorate both of these issues.

In a densely packed wood, you will have to consider whether you should thin the trees. This is not a job for the faint hearted, involving hard graft, hard cash or both, as ideally the stump and roots should be removed as well, especially if you intend to grow any understorey trees and shrubs which

Notice how the sheltering background trees in Marion Jarvie's Toronto garden have had their lower branches removed to a height of about 30 ft. (10 m) with no ill effect.

could be subject to fungal attack from the rotting stumps at some future stage. The easy decision is to first remove dead, dying and weak trees or branches. Then it becomes either more exciting or challenging, depending on your outlook, so give the next stage a lot of thought before plunging in. Every situation will be different and there are no rules. Do you thin the trees evenly throughout the wood leaving just the best specimens, or leave clumps of closely spaced trunks and open up glades between them, or some combination of both?

Pruning up the canopy

In more open woods or if your property has just a few mature trees, you can still increase light levels by removing the lower branches on some or all of the trees. How high you do this depends to a certain extent on the existing size of the trees. As a general rule, the taller the tree, the higher the branches that can be removed. However, you must always remember to keep the symmetry of the tree; too high and the finished effect can look like a small lollipop on a long stick! Because conifers generally have a greater light-blocking canopy, they are likely to need pruning higher than deciduous trees—but there is no limit to how high skirting up can be practiced. Provided the tree is strong and healthy and the branches are cut when the sap is not rising (that is, when the trees are dormant) no harm should come to the tree. Clearly there can be some cost involved, as you may need the help of a tree surgeon or arborist. I personally do not feel comfortable removing branches above about 15 ft. (4.5 m) without calling in expert help.

Preparing the soil

I used to believe that woodlanders were pretty easy-going with regards to soil fertility given that they are able to cope with thin soils and tree roots, but in recent years I have come to the conclusion that the opposite is true and actually they are quite greedy feeders. To maintain good growth and healthy plants, an annual mulch is, if not a necessity, then highly desirable. Even wood anemones (*Anemone nemorosa*) that appear in the wild to revel atop seemingly inhospitable roadside banks, are transformed when given a nourishing annual mulch of organic matter. In their natural optimum conditions of deciduous trees, the woods and all the plants that grow in them are treated to an autumnal mulch of fallen leaves. The spring-flowering bulbs and perennials get first option each year to exploit this bounty before the trees suck it dry of nutrients through late spring and summer. Without

The soil level around some of the trees at Heronswood, on Bainbridge Island, Washington, was successfully raised to accommodate lower-level plants. However, this technique should be used with caution.

These *Magnolia ×soulangeana* were deliberately planted close together so their lichen-covered trunks become ever more imposing with age. The original bulbs beneath, now self-seeding, were planted at the same time as the magnolias and include anemones and *Erythronium revolutum*.

this annual injection of organic matter, the health and vigour of the woodland flora would quite quickly deteriorate. As in nature, so too in the garden.

As long as you can reasonably push a spade or fork partway at least into most of the ground beneath your trees to turn the ensuing soil, then you don't need to do much more than clear the ground of weeds. Ground clearance is best carried out in the winter months, after which you can spread a thick a layer of organic matter and then plant in early spring. From then on, apply a feeding mulch when the plants show signs of diminishing vigour or on a regular basis through the winter months.

If you do have trees with shallow, aggressive roots, one way of preparing the ground for planting is to raise the soil level above the existing roots. This is a risky practice, though, and I would not attempt it around an especially

Fritillaria meleagris

Good self-seeders

- *Allium triquetrum**
- *Chionodoxa*
- *Corydalis linstowiana*
- *Corydalis cheilanthifolia*
- *Corydalis shimienensis*
- *Claytonia perfoliata**
- *Crocus tommasinianus*
- *Cyclamen coum*
- *Cyclamen hederifolium*
- *Eranthis*
- *Erythronium revolutum*
- *Erythronium oregonum*
- *Fritillaria meleagris*
- *Geranium asphodeloides*
- *Hyacinthoides non-scripta**
- *Meconopsis cambrica**
- *Narcissus bulbocodium*
- *Narcissus pseudonarcissus**
- *Primula vulgaris*
- *Ranunculus ficaria**
- *Scilla campanulatus**

*For large-scale plantings

valuable tree (like a magnolia), nor would I pile any soil up around the tree trunks at all. I would restrict myself to adding soil to a depth no greater than perhaps 1 ft. (30 cm) around the outer fringes of the tree's spread, petering out to nothing around the trunk. The tree roots will eventually grow up into this added soil, so at best you are only gaining a few precious years of breathing space in which to be able to plant with a trowel without breaking your wrists. However, it will provide you with the benefit of being able to introduce a wider range of species (including some woody plants) than would be possible by mere seed scattering alone and allows a much greater control over the finished plant combinations. This is the method I used in the "bulb meadow" at the Garden House.

If you have established trees that make underplanting impossible, you still have options, provided light can reach the soil surface. I have very successfully established carpets of erythroniums by regularly scattering their seeds in situ. Virtually any woodlander that naturally spreads by self-seeding could be tried in a similar situation. For instance, I have often grown primroses and chionodoxa among the roots of established magnolias.

Creating woodland conditions

Suppose you want to create a woodland garden, but you have little natural shade? This was the situation at Wildside, where I used a number of techniques to create two acres of woodland mounds, hollows, ponds and pathways. Many of these techniques can be used in smaller plots, even tiny spaces. The primary goal is to create the right kind of shady habitat, using the layered woodland components of canopy, understorey and underplanting.

Shaping the land

Land forming is the practice of reshaping the contours of the ground, in this case to create various habitats to suit the needs of different plants. On a large scale it may well require planning permission, as was the case with the almost epic scale on the whole of Wildside's four-acre site, where I moved over 70,000 tonnes of soil and shillet (a local name for the underlying semi-degraded slate stone) to create gullies, hills, pathways and ponds. Some of the banks created on the site are nearly 40 ft. (12 m) high.

Although it is possible to dig these by hand (especially if you are Swedish and called Peter Korn) the task is made much easier if you have the use of a caterpillar-tracked digger or swing-shovel (a piece of equipment that makes tree-stump removal much easier as well). The process is very simple. I hired, in fortnightly chunks, a 3.5-tonne digger and 3-tonne dumper truck, both of which I drove myself. After 70,000 tonnes you can become quite proficient as a digger operator. I removed the topsoil from the entire site and put it to one side. In some places I dug into the stoney substrate to form ponds and valley floors and then piled this removed material up on the valley sides to

This image shows some of the newly formed banks at Wildside the first winter after they were planted. These banks range in height from 5–6 ft. (1.5–2 m), with pathways winding between their dune-like shapes.

create the hills. When the desired heights and contours were reached, I brought the topsoil back onto the reshaped hills, typically to a depth of 1 ft. (30 cm).

Due to the relatively low angle of the spring sun in the southern sky, I reasoned that creating raised banks even as high as 6 ft. (2 m) with small shrubs and trees planted on their summits would provide enough shade for low-growing woodlanders to thrive on the relatively long, shaded northern sides of the banks. This shaded planting area is twice as large when a tree is on a raised mound rather than on flat ground; including the sunny southern side there is a 25 percent overall increase in planting area compared to a level site. Even in summer these northern slopes are significantly cooler than those facing south.

Because we receive up to 60 in. (1.5 m) of rain per year and have a moisture-retentive loam as our soil type, underlain with the shillet, this land-forming technique provides that elusive combination so beloved of garden writers of moisture-retentive yet free-draining soil. Another benefit of the process is that the banks raise up the planting area, so that flowers are closer to your face for an all-important closer look. This has worked spectacularly well with Chinese epimediums, erythroniums, trilliums and many other choice woodlanders, especially for those whose down-curved flowers are often difficult to see without crouching.

By planting this *Erythronium citrinum* × *E. hendersonii* hybrid on the top of a 3-ft. (1-m) bank, I can admire the handsome foliage and internal flower details without having to bend down or turn up the flowers to peer inside.

These banks of similar height at Wildside were sculpted from one of the piles of topsoil created when I first cleared the field. Planted with wisterias and dwarf shrubs, the spaces between are homes for spring-flowering bulbs, especially erythroniums.

Shaded banks

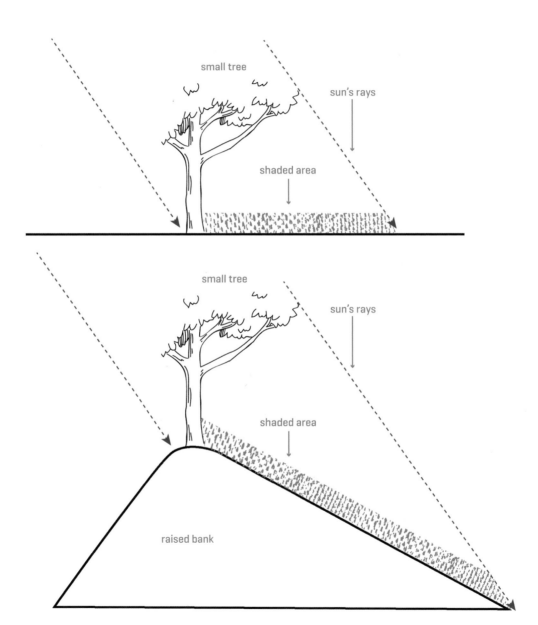

small tree

sun's rays

shaded area

small tree

sun's rays

shaded area

raised bank

Planting trees

In addition to land forming, the most obvious way to create good conditions for woodland plants is to plant some trees. The choice of shade-providing tree will depend on the characteristics mentioned in chapter 1, as well as its suitability for your region. Because the form, foliage and bark of trees vary so much, you have plenty of options to create whatever look you hope to achieve, whether an Asian-inspired mood, the feel of a southern Californian coastal glade, an Antipodean eucalyptus or cordyline planting, a South African atmosphere, a Mediterranean look or a more traditional woodland atmosphere. Your garden's overall style will also influence your choices.

For instance, if you prefer a more formal style of garden, you could plant trees on a regular grid system, spacing them depending on the spread of the individual trees, much like an adapted commercial forestry plantation. The fewer the varieties of trees used the greater the uniformity. In the grounds of the University of Alnarp in Sweden, the plantation plantings of various species, notably *Cercidiphyllum japonicum* and *Metasequoia glypstroboides*, are a good example of this effect. Both these species are blessed with fine-fissured trunks and elegant form. Underneath and between these trees a whole range of woodland perennials and bulbs would find a congenial home. In this case a random underplanting would contrast strongly with the geometry of the tree spacings.

Another way to use vertical elements is to follow the lead of familiar Italian and other Mediterranean gardens, renowned for the pencil-thin Italian cypresses punctuating the landscape. Clearly these conifers, if you can grow them, will provide virtually no shade but other fastigiate plants could provide the same effect. Again the metasequoia, for example, repeated at wider but still regular spacings within a linear formal design would be a good choice for year-round interest, as would silver birch trees.

The repetition of a planting of a single tree species need not be restricted to fastigiate trees. Flowering trees like dogwoods, eucryphias and magnolias as well as those grown primarily for foliage such as Japanese maples, hollies and medium-sized conifers would make exciting choices, each one creating a very different atmosphere. I can see this working with virtually any medium-sized tree, not just vaguely pyramidal-shaped ones. The same design principle can apply in quite small gardens, with the use of smaller trees or large shrubs, with scaled-down perennials planted beneath them. If round-topped trees were used the effect would be more like an apple orchard that was underplanted with shade-loving plants.

A different type of atmosphere can be created for a woodland space with a limited number of species, repeated but mixed together. One such combination I am very happy with here at Wildside involves cercidiphyllums, *Amelanchier* and *Magnolia ×loebneri* 'Merrill' underplanted with *Corylopsis pauciflora*. At any time of the year they are a very happy grouping with complimentary combinations of habit, leaf shape, trunk colours and with sequential flowering and autumn colour. With a little judicious skirting-up, and despite being planted very close together, even in midsummer, the small leaf size of all these plants allows sufficient light through to the ground to allow a community of perennials and bulbs to flourish there.

Creating miniature woodlands

In one area of the garden I have used land forming and tree planting to turn a long-held ambition into a reality: to create a free-standing wisteria copse underplanted with some of the aristocrats of the woodland world. This concept could be applied with other trees and shrubs in almost any garden situation.

To create the wisteria woods, I created raised banks up to 4 ft. (1.2 m) high by digging paths through one of the large piles of topsoil (that has originally been stripped off the site) and which had been left to consolidate for at least two years. After this time, they were settled and solid enough to be sculpted with spade and wheelbarrow into finished shapes, leaving narrow paths winding through the gullies between the banks. On top of these, I planted wisterias in variety, but mostly of *Wisteria floribunda* types (although it works with any wisteria), each with a strong stake to support the trunk. My personal choice is to use metal stakes which are narrower and less noticeable, but wooden supports would function just as well. Because the wisterias are astonishingly vigorous in their root growth, they quickly help to stabilize the banks, but it also means that they must be underplanted as soon as possible. There are enough gaps between the roots to support a wide array of plants but I would not recommend plants that will require regular digging and division, such as double primroses.

Having long-held unfulfilled plans for a particular planting concept can make one reluctant to change or modify when the plan starts to become a reality. I had always envisaged these wisterias to be individually distinct, some growing almost sideways, some multi-trunked so that I ended up with a very diverse but natural-looking copse with the wisteria growing

A grove of aspens undercarpeted with camas clearly demonstrates the value of trunks as a year-round feature. The random spacings and trunk diameters and angles all influence the apparent naturalness of the wood.

In hotter, sunnier climates than my own, olive trees underplanted with agapanthus are a good choice to create a woodland with echoes of the Mediterranean.

no higher than 6 ft. (2 m), rather than a series of similar half-standard type specimens. This would have worked if I grew only spring-flowering bulbs underneath the wisterias, but I wanted to extend the textures, foliage colours and flowering season by underplanting with a range of species and plant types below the canopy—almost certainly a case of a spoilt child wanting too much! I found almost immediately that the lowest branches of the wisterias droop too much with the weight of their own flowers and foliage, compromising the growth of the plants beneath. To allow for the growth of dwarf shrubs in particular, I have had to raise the canopy higher than I envisioned. Another option to maintain the natural feel would be to revert to the original idea and remove the understorey shrubs, simplifying the plant palette in the process. Flexibility is crucial to allow almost any concept to evolve.

Apart from this unforeseen need to remove the lower branches, the maintenance of these wisterias is pretty standard. The general shape I aim for is that of a mature oak tree. To encourage this, I remove the strong growing shoots that spring from the main trunk without exception, along with those that spring from below ground. These latter ones should be cut off as low as possible to prevent re-growth. Once the plants have reached their required mature height, I remove any vertical extension growth from the higher regions of the plant, and generally prune back at the end of summer to three buds. My aim is to avoid any spiky vertical shoots so the plant does not look like it has a Mohawk haircut. To encourage growth in a specific direction, you can shorten back in the desired directions by any amount, leaving the attached branch growing at an angle of no more than thirty degrees above the horizontal. (The weight of the ensuing growth will then lower this branch closer to horizontal.) I also remove growths that are coiling around each other as these are not conducive to creating a natural tree shape.

This planting technique can be used to reproduce on a small scale the look and feel of native woodlands using plants other than wisteria. For example, the more dome-shaped Japanese maples (as opposed to vase-shaped) have vaguely the same outline as hawthorn bushes (*Crataegus*), hamamelis as hazel bushes (*Corylus*) and magnolias bring to mind ash trees (*Fraxinus*) when not in leaf. Slow-growing dwarf conifers are another option, pruned to mimic their larger cousins. Even as few as three such plants spaced so their branches are not quite touching can create a shaded planting space between them for growing smaller woodlanders, especially plants like cyclamen which thrive in the drier conditions among the tree roots. My preference is to repeat the

The wisteria grove at Wildside was created by planting the shrubby vines on raised banks to create variously shaded conditions on the sloping sides of the banks.

same plant in groups, which gives a unity to the design, and for a shrub or tree habit that is at first upright, then arching outwards. This particular shape enables maximum planting space below, coupled with maximum shading.

In small spaces, the choice of which tree to use as a shade specimen is even more crucial. It must be slow growing, otherwise you will be forever pruning the tree and its natural shape is likely to disappear. However, for instant shade, you will need to plant fairly mature specimens, or else grow sun-loving plants around them for a few years with the intention of changing over to shade-lovers as these small trees mature. The dwarf-growing *Prunus incisa* 'Kojo-no-mai' would be a good choice, as would the compact-growing *Cercidiphyllum japonicum* 'Boyd's Dwarf' and *Betula pendula* 'Trost's Dwarf' or any of the very slow-growing Japanese maple varieties such as 'Corallinum', 'Katsura' or 'Little Princess' (all of which rarely grow taller than 5 ft. [1.5 m]). Many of the slow-growing conifers would also be suitable, such as *Chamaecyparis* and a few of the other *Chamaecyparis pisifera* forms, like the 'Filifera' group. If the conifer grows slowly and has a graceful habit, you can gradually remove the lower branches to reveal the characterful trunk.

In a larger garden, *Magnolia stellata* does the job really well. Stepping up a size again I have used the summer-flowering *M. sieboldii* and *M. wilsonii* to create mini-copses with about twelve specimens in each group. A single *Acer griseum*

This *Chamaecyparis* has been pruned by thinning many of the lower branches and the resulting shape resembles a Scots pine. Here, the confier is about 6 ft. (2 m) high but it would work equally well if it was half this height.

The slow-growing *Betula pendula* 'Trost's Dwarf', if irregularly repeated, would be a good choice for creating a miniature woodland.

is an asset to any garden, but plant several of them in a widely spaced grouping and you have some very desirable woodland planting room in between, with the added benefit of the maple's wonderful trunks with their peeling cinnamon-coloured bark. Larger again, a group of *Magnolia soulangeana* is going to need a sizeable garden to do them justice.

These *Magnolia stellata* are six or seven years old and have reached a size where I can gradually remove the lower branches every year to allow more light to reach the bulbs and other woodlanders beneath.

Creating shade with shrubs

It may be that you already have existing large shrubs that could, with a little pruning, do this job of providing shade for underplantings. It doesn't matter if the plant is single- or multi-trunked, nor how long the trunks are, as long as they are more or less upright for the first few feet or so before they spread outwards. The main goal is to carefully remove some of the lowest branches to introduce some light to the ground beneath the shrub's canopy and to reveal the often hidden beauty of the branch structure. The commonest mistake to make attempting this is to remove too many branches too quickly. Start with the bare minimum and then carefully consider over days or weeks if necessary before removing any others. Being too saw-happy to start with can result in a specimen more lollipop than is graceful and it may take several years to regain balance between foliage mass and overall size.

This treatment can work very well on shrubs as small as evergreen azaleas and dwarf rhododendrons to large shrubs such as philadelphus, viburnums, most conifers and pieris. Smaller-leaved camellias with a more spreading habit and large rhododendrons with cinnamon-coloured branches would be a prime target. However, if your main aim though is to create more planting space for woodlanders below these shrubs rather than improve the aesthetics of the specimen itself, give a little consideration beforehand to the density of the shrub's root system, just as you would for shade trees. It would be counter-productive having done all this agonizing over the pruning if the root system is so dense you are unable to plant anything.

Building structures

There is no need to use only plants to create the shaded conditions required for a woodland garden. We all know the beds on the north side of our houses are cooler (at least in the northern hemisphere) and so a good place for many woodland plants. Any structure in the garden of sufficient height will create similar planting conditions. Walls or sections of walls about 6 ft. (2 m) high could provide perfect growing conditions on all but any south-facing aspects right up to the wall base. A similar-sized hedge will provide the same shade but because you must leave some space along the hedge for maintenance, you will not be able to plant anything adjacent to it.

A series of concrete block walls coated with coloured mortar along the lines of the shapes in the diagram (page 55) produce focal point, shelter and partial shade. If the walls are built at different angles to each other they will each in turn provide shade as the sun arcs across the sky. Add a pair of small trees of graceful form such as Japanese maples, species cherries or crabapples, or silver birches and you have a modern design with perfect conditions for woodland plants. Not only will the walls cast strong shadows bringing the drama of light and shade into the area, but any plant with a strong architectural shape planted in front of them will cast exciting shadows onto the walls themselves. The same concept could be used with wooden trellises or posts and fencing rails and then covered with climbing plants. You wouldn't have the shadows on the structure, but you would get dappled sunlight coming through the woodwork and the climbers offer new possibilities for unusual plant combinations with the surrounding shade-loving plants.

In Dan Hinkley and Robert Jones' new garden at Windcliff near Seattle, a tiny area next to the house shows how with a little ingenuity a small shady space can be turned into a very desirable spot.

These pseudo-adobe walls in Robin Hopper's garden inspired those in my own courtyard, where I have managed to create sections of garden devoted to woodland plants where there was previously no shade at all.

The fusion of Asian and Western styles in Robin Hopper's garden is well illustrated by this seat he designed and built. It works well as a focal point in more natural plantings. My version of this is already planned for Wildside.

Walls and fences create not only shade but if sited away from the garden boundary can break up the garden into smaller units. This is demonstrated in Robin Hopper and Judi Dyelle's garden in Victoria, Canada, where clever use of walls and other structures break up the garden space into smaller more intimate units.

If you live in an area where stone is locally available, you can build dry stone walls, infilling with good soil in place of mortar. Inspection of any stone-built walls or banks in the countryside around you will quickly show you the best way to build with the local stone or rocks. For instance, most of the field hedges in the southwest of the United Kingdom are supported by 3 ft. (1 m) stone walls on either side and these often become homes to thriving colonies of woodland plants such as ferns and primroses on their shady sides. If you do intend to plant into new stone walls you are building, remember the top surface of all the individual stones should angle back towards the central base of the wall so that any falling rain penetrates into the structure rather than away from it. If you fail to do this the plants positioned on the sides of the wall will likewise fail in the first prolonged dry spell as the centre of a dry stone wall can be very dry indeed. A dry stone wall that hasn't been purpose-built for plants will be able to support very little plant growth because of this.

With a little imagination you can find planting opportunities in all sorts of unlikely places. Virtually any human-made structure can provide shade. A cantilevered deck, especially one emanating from the first floor of a building, would provide excellent conditions for hard-core shade-demanding plants below it, provided not too many chemicals are used to clean the decking. After all, if the gaps were a little wider on the decking, you would essentially have a "lath house", the woodland plant equivalent of a 5-star hotel. Expand the gap between the top timbers much wider and you arrive at a structure very like a pergola, under which the dappled light is perfect for a wide range of woodland plants.

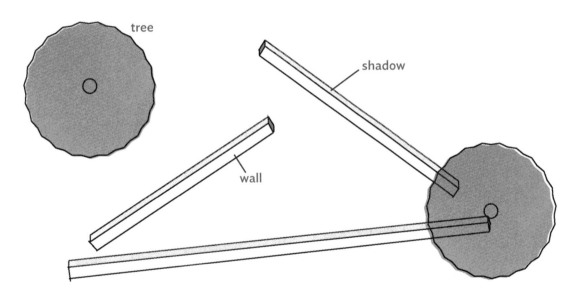

N

As the sun travels across this plot from east to west, the shade created by the walls and the trees means that all the planting space gets good light, but none is in full sun for more than three or four hours each day.

Dodecatheon clevelandii ssp. *insulare* growing on grassy slopes on the Temblor Range in central California.

Special Situations

Many variables other than just tree cover affect the growth of woodland plants. Whether your site is grassy, sandy or moist will influence what it may be possible to plant. Each of these habitats can be transformed into a woodland garden, but will require some preparation and an understanding of the site conditions. As always, it can help to review how plants grow in their native habitats to gain some insight into how they may grow in the garden. If your desire is to have a low-maintenance garden in a small space, this too can be accomplished, by carefully choosing the right plants for the spot.

Grassy woodlands

Traditional fruit orchard trees have branches no lower than about 6 ft. (2 m), presumably either because the livestock grazing beneath them eat all the lower shoots or to allow for easier harvesting. The land below is usually covered with grass, grazing for pigs and sheep that finish off the windfall fruit as well. The result of this combination is surprisingly good growing conditions for many shade-loving plants.

In fact, some woodland species—like arisaemas, lilies, primulas and podophyllums can grow in grass in their native habitats. *Primula sieboldii*, for instance, grows in tall grass meadows in its native Japan. So it is very possible to create a woodland garden in a semi-shaded grassy area. But before considering what plants might be suitable for growing in such a meadow, you first need to decide how you will manage the grassy area through the year.

A typical maintenance schedule would be to leave the area unmown and completely undisturbed from midwinter until midsummer, at which point the grass is cut. If you are growing only spring bulbs, the annual mowing can be in early summer, perhaps about six weeks after the last bulbs have flowered. If the grassed area includes wildflowers which usually flower in late spring and early summer, you will need to delay the first cut until late midsummer. After cutting, the mown grass should be left to dry in the sun in situ for a few days to allow seeds of flowering plants to fall to the ground. Then take away the hay, and when the grass has greened up again and started to grow you can regularly mow until the end of the year. If autumn-flowering bulbs are planted, such as colchicums, autumn crocus or *Cyclamen hederifolium*, the more complicated the timing of mowing becomes and you will need an intimate knowledge of when the plants are likely to appear above ground in your conditions. If you are establishing a meadow, I suggest you start with plants that flower during roughly one season of the year, such as the spring, and then gradually extend the planting through the summer and autumn.

A limiting factor for growing perennials in grass is whether they tolerate being mown later in the season. Many spring- and early-summer-flowering perennials can be happily cut down after flowering. After all, alpine hay meadows are regularly cut back after flowering and they remain species-rich. Those perennials most likely to survive mowing send up new shoots from or below ground level. Others which form raised crowns or low clumps for much or all of the year from which their flowering stems rise, such as *Silene dioica* (pink campion) are unlikely to thrive. Similarly, those perennials which spend their dormant season as prominent above-ground buds, such as many hostas, are not likely to survive the mower, although you may be able to place some plants in pockets cut an inch or so below ground level.

Something else to consider when adapting an existing piece of grassland is the vigour of the grass. The key factor for flower and species-rich meadows is thin grass. If you want plants to seed and naturalize through the sward then thin grass is essential. Light must be able to reach the seedlings when they are in growth or they are likely doomed, even in the unlikely event they had managed to germinate in the first place. In temperate climates the grass species are the first plants to spring into growth as the daylight hours begin to lengthen. By the time flowering perennials and bulbs start to emerge the grass can already be quite long, cutting out light and eventually smothering those flowering plants. In thick grass there is little chance of light reaching the ground to encourage the development of seedlings at any time of

Bird's foot trefoil (*Lotus corniculatus*) and ox-eye daisies form patches of early summer colour in a meadow garden. A succession of bulbous plants dot the intervening grass spaces from early spring through to autumn.

Erythronium 'White Beauty' growing happily in short turf. Other erythroniums, such as *E. oregonum*, have self-seeded into grassy areas at Wildside.

the year. So first you need to eliminate the vigorous grass species. How you choose to do this depends on your bank balance and the time scale, and whether or not you prefer to use organic methods. Stripping off the topsoil to reduce fertility is sometimes recommended but seems to me to be both expensive, time consuming and is unlikely to benefit the exciting plants I eventually want to be there.

You can eradicate vigorous grass and troublesome perennial weeds by spraying it with a herbicide and then reseeding with dwarfer grass species. You can also dramatically reduce the vigour of coarse grass within a single season with the use of growth-retarding sprays. In the United Kingdom, the semi-parasitic yellow rattle (*Rhinanthus minor*) can be sown as an organic method to reduce grass vigour. The best method to get this established is to rake fresh seed into newly mown turf. An alternative method is to try and obtain some hay from known meadows where yellow rattle is present and spread this over the tightly shaved grass in midsummer. You may even find that you introduce native orchids into the meadow at the same time if they were present in the original hay meadow.

At the top of many people's lists for growing in grass would be orchids, the choice of species depending on the pH of your soil. On my acid soil I am content to be mostly restricted to *Dactylorhiza* species, especially *D. grandis* 'Blackthorn Strain'. I grow as many different forms of the "dacs"

Woodlanders for grassy spots

- *Ajuga*
- *Allium carinatum* ssp. *pulchellum*
- *Anemone pavonina*
- *Cyclamen coum*
- *Cyclamen hederifolium*
- *Erythronium*
- *Geranium asphodeloides*
- *Gladiolus palustris*

- *Narcissus*
- *Ranunculus acris* (especially the pale yellow form 'Citrinus')
- *Saxifraga granulata*
- *Tulipa sprengeri*
- *Tulipa sylvestris*
- And most of the self-seeders listed on page 43.

The scented yellow *Tulipa sylvestris* in a Swedish meadow is one of a limited number of tulips that will colonize grassy environments. In more shaded areas it flowers less prolifically.

Dactylorhiza ✕*grandis* 'Blackthorn Strain' grows happily in the grass to around 18 in. (45 cm). In good growing conditions in well-prepared beds with no grass competition this orchid can reach 30 in. (70 cm) tall.

as possible in beds around my grassy orchard in the hope and expectation they will cross-fertilize and start seeding themselves into the grass. After three or four years of using yellow rattle to reduce the vigour of the sward the orchids are now doing just that and I hope at some time in the future to see hundreds of them in various shades of pink and white studding our turf.

Spring- and early-summer-flowering bulbs of all kinds are worth planting in a grassy meadow, and many more will succeed than you might think. For instance, you would not expect *Anemone pavonina* from the hotter conditions of the Mediterranean to find a congenial home in the grass. Yet in the wild it is found in the partial shade of olive groves and vineyards as well as grassy places and it appears equally at home in similar conditions in our cooler, wetter climate. Similarly *A. heldreichii* grows in stony and rocky places in its native Crete, but can be successfully grown under apple trees. Soils with good drainage are much more likely to succeed with plants like these anemones and *Cyclamen coum* and *C. hederifolium* in the shadier spots. *Tulipa sprengeri* and *T. sylvestris* do not seem to require such good drainage as many other tulips. The plants included here should do well on many soils—but the real fun when you have spare plants is experimenting with almost anything to find out which do well in your garden.

Growing in sandy soil

I have successfully grown sun-loving plants in 8 in. (20 cm) of pure sand, but I would not have thought attempting it with woodlanders until I met Peter Korn from Sweden. In a very passable impression of Superman (if you doubt my words check his website, www.peterkornstradgard.se) he has created a staggering landscape in an impoverished five-acre spruce wood, sculpting rocky banks by hand to a height of 30 ft. (10 m) and covering them with with at least 8 in. (20 cm) of coarse sand. The sand he uses ranges from 8-mm grit down and has something approaching the consistency of demerara sugar. Peter plants everything in these sand beds, including woodlanders, and then top-dresses the surface with a mixture of various-sized stones, which gives a wonderfully natural-looking effect. Peter's first love is

In this section of one of Peter Korn's recently planted sand beds, the skillful placing of rocks of all sizes, from boulders to pea shingle, as a surface layer to the beds gives a very natural appearance. If you took out the plant labels it would be difficult to tell the difference from a mountain slope in the wild.

Cypripedium ventricosum growing in a moist section of a well-established sand bed. Native grasses and mosses create a more natural-looking backdrop.

Meconopsis 'Lingholm' is happily perennial in another section of Peter Korn's garden, growing in nothing but 18 in. (45cm) of sand. In this area spring water constantly seeps through the lower levels of the sand.

for alpine plants, many of which require excellent drainage, but included in this general group are a large number of highly desirable woodland plants. His phenomenal success at growing these difficult plants so they appear to be completely natural is testament to his skills as a grower and his artistic eye as well as his ingenuity.

Ian Young, an expert grower of bulbous plants in Scotland, says of Peter's bewildering capacity for hard work, "Given a choice of twenty navvies or Peter Korn, I would opt for Peter every time." This may beg the question, why bother going to such lengths? The answer is twofold. Firstly, if you get the consistency and sufficient depth of the sand right, many difficult-to-grow plants can thrive and still retain their natural character and habit. Secondly and equally importantly, there is much less of the weeding which is such a contentious issue in ordinary soil especially with smaller plants, and what few weeds do take hold are easily removed with just a finger and thumb. Given the large amount of weeding needed to keep alpines and smaller woodland treasures looking good in ordinary garden conditions, this method devised by Peter enables him to indulge his passion for these smaller plants on a grand scale with an almost unimaginably large number of taxa (he says over 14,000 different taxa, which is more than most botanic gardens). I love the sheer bravura of his efforts and would like to replicate them on a similar scale in my own garden but know that without a ready supply of cheap sand the costs would be prohibitive. Nonetheless I am convinced of the principles involved and determined to incorporate some smaller sand beds for special plants somewhere in my own garden.

One of the advantages of sand beds is that moisture is always present 4–6 in. (10–15 cm) down in the sand, so although the top layer may be very dry (discouraging weed germination) even in summer there will always be some moisture at greater depths. Sand is also relatively nutrient poor, so the root systems of plants growing there are very extensive because they must grow to search out nutrients. This combination results in many higher altitude plants staying in character with relatively compact growth above ground and large root systems below ground. For those plants that require more moisture than a standard sand bed could provide, you can build a system that mimics glacial moraines where water percolates under the stones to provide plant roots with access to running water.

Growing on peat

Constructing beds using sphagnum moss blocks is another method that can allow you to grow smaller, more precious woodlanders in optimum conditions. Clearly the use of peat in any form is a contentious issue these days. In Sweden, peat blocks are considered a renewable, sustainable resource and the vast majority are used for power generation, as elsewhere in Europe. In

Shortia soldanelloides growing in the peat blocks at the Gothenburg Botanical Garden. This treasure only grows 6 in. (15 cm) high so would be easily overcrowded unless grown with equally small plants

One of the hardiest pleiones is *Pleione yunnanensis*. Here it is growing unprotected in a peat block in Gothenburg surrounded by moss (*Polytrichum* sp.) which springs unsolicited from the peat blocks.

North America, peat is rarely used for power generation but Canada is the largest producer of horticultural peat in the world. Clearly there are strong cases to be made for both sides but one has to wonder whether two of the most celebrated botanic gardens in the world, Edinburgh and Gothenburg, would still feature beds built with peat blocks if there were not valid arguments for their continued use.

I have used large sphagnum moss Swedish peat blocks since being prompted to do so thirty years ago by a gardener from the Gothenburg Botanical Garden. Soon after, and long before the furore over peat use became widespread, I bought a container load with the aim of making a large peat garden. I have successfully used some of the blocks to form the banks

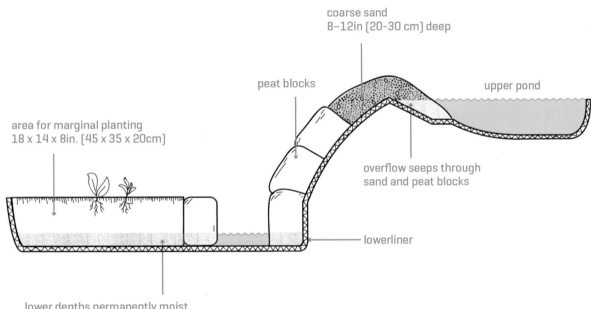

This modification of a wet sand bed uses large peat blocks, 18 × 14 × 8 in. (45 × 35 × 20 cm). The overflow from the top pond seeps through the sand and the peat blocks before reaching the lower pond, where the lower depths of the marginal planting area are kept permanently moist. Ideally a peat bed planting would be lightly shaded by nearby trees but if the stream banks were in full shade this arrangement could provide a very good home to the difficult but very special petiolarid primulas, most notably the *Primula whitei* of my long-cherished dreams. Some gardeners in the Netherlands grow pleiones in similar peat block banks they call "turf walls".

of a small stream section in a water garden. Their amazing water-holding capacity means they act as sponges, providing a well-aerated yet moisture-retentive rooting medium, perfect for many of the choicest woodlanders, such as moisture-loving cassiopes, epigaeas, orchids and shortias.

Clearly to construct a garden bed along these lines is a time-consuming and expensive process, but the range of choice woodlanders that could be grown there is a mouth-watering prospect, and if nothing else it shows the lengths to which some people will go to provide near-ideal conditions for their plants. Edinburgh Botanic Garden has recently rebuilt its peat garden using Swedish peat blocks as low retaining walls and then back-filled with a leafy, woodsy soil. When the peat blocks are fully hydrated, they can be planted with the most special woodland plants, such as cassiopes, epigaeas, gentians, shortias, phyllodoces, nomocharis, dwarf rhododendrons, ×phylliopsis and many others. The late Alfred Evans looked after the peat beds at Edinburgh for twenty-five years and his now out-of-print book *The Peat Garden and its Plants* is still the best reference work for those gardeners who wish to find out more about this specialist branch of woodland gardening.

Growing in moist woodlands

I can trace my own longing for a cool and shady stream and its planting potential to a television programme many years ago which featured a Scottish woodland garden with a burn cascading through it. The steep banks on either side were completely covered in one of the difficult petiolarid group of ice-blue species primulas, either *Primula sonchifolia* or *P. whitei*, in full flower. In this situation, the plants' habit of occasionally dropping their fat dormant buds in the winter months resulted in the buds falling down the bank and taking root, spreading the colony further. The effect was magical and I am still trying to emulate this in some small way.

There are not many shade-loving plants that actually grow in water. Classic water plants like water lilies and water iris will flower and stay in character better when given full sun. Many streamside plants such as candelabra primulas also need some sunlight to flower well. If you are considering building a pond, I don't recommend you position it in a shady location if these familiar water lovers are important to you. If you already have a natural pond or stream in your garden running through shaded areas, determine the patterns of sun and shade throughout the growing season before devising a planting scheme.

Hostas, *Euphorbia griffithii* 'Fireglow', *Campanula lactiflora* and the spikes of *Tellima grandiflora* bask in the dappled light and cool moist conditions of a Devon garden. *Milium effusum* 'Aureum' provides a pale yellow hazy background.

In midsummer, Wildside is bursting with bloom. This view of the stream garden runs from southeast (foreground) to northwest (distance). The cooler conditions on the left bank provide good homes for woodlanders. As the trees grow and cast more shade the plantings will be modified to include more shade-tolerant species. (This is the reverse view of the central image on page 17.)

Some plants will tolerate growing in a partially shaded pond, such as golden creeping jenny, *Lysimachia nummularia* 'Aurea', the golden sedge, *Carex elata* 'Aurea' and the evil-smelling (at least to my nose) *Houttuynia cordata* (even the variegated form 'Chameleon' is an extremely vigorous spreader, so introduce it to your borders at your peril or plant it in a pot below the water and keep an eye on it). There are also foliage plants that are happy alongside a shaded pond. Hostas and most ferns love it there. If the shade is cast by deciduous trees and shrubs, you can plant any of the spring-flowering perennials and bulbs. If sunlight penetrates for a few hours each day the choice becomes so extensive it includes most of the plants mentioned in this book.

Stream banks are a favoured location for many woodland plants, as nearly all woodland plants like cool conditions, and growing alongside a stream or pond is bound to make any plant that likes it cool feel more at home. Clearly the larger the area of water or the more fast flowing, the more humidity will be in the air, which is even better for the plants growing close by. There are also the benefits of drainage of the bank itself, a constant source of water for any deeper roots. Astilbes, hostas, rodgersias, *Iris ensata* and many other perennials are in their element here. If you are trying to recreate these conditions with a lined pond remember that often the soil outside the liner can be very dry. In my own water garden I have sunk the ponds into the ground to create banks running down to the water and made sure the soil on them also continued into the pond itself. This creates a "wicking" effect giving plants above the opportunity to send their roots down to the water.

Small woodland gardens

The layered approach of a woodland garden, with trees, shrubs and ground-level plants blended together, allows you to fit more plants into a small space. It works on a grand scale, as has been shown at Winterthur Gardens in Delaware, but is a template that works equally as well on a much smaller plot. Many of the smaller gardens I was shown and admired in Toronto and Vancouver, Canada, were basically woodland gardens planted along these all-inclusive lines—woodland in atmosphere but not necessarily full of what we generally call woodland plants. Marion and Alex Jarvie's garden in Toronto is a particularly inspirational example, showing how a dedicated plantsperson can make a garden that looks great for an unfeasibly long stretch of the year, almost year round in fact, in a climate that doesn't allow you to garden through the frigid winter months.

Sue Moss has brought a sense of sunshine and light into an implausibly small narrow space in her Seattle garden with the use of golden-leaved shade-loving plants.

Although I prefer a natural style in my large garden, this is not as easy to pull off in a small space, and the wider variety of plants you include in a smaller garden the less natural it is likely to look. You can lend a small garden an authentic woodland feel by ensuring there are tall trees, either as a backdrop or as one or two specimens. These trees provide valuable shade and their trunks and high canopy lend structure to the whole garden. It is similar to the surprisingly powerful effect that framing has on a painting or photograph, excluding extraneous details and concentrating the eye on the picture itself (or on the garden in this instance).

Low-growing woodlanders can play an important part in even tiny spaces, perhaps alongside paths into or parallel to the house. Look for areas on the north side of the house or other structures that can be planted. In such small spaces the use of containers, works of art and the interplay between hard surfaces and plant material becomes more important.

Alongside a path is one area where very small plants can be appreciated. Here, white *Rhodohypoxis baurii* 'Pictus' carpets the ground below *Roscoea cautleyoides* 'Kew Beauty' and self-seeding *Meconopsis cambrica*.

In this Philadelphia garden, exotic and tender foliage plants and even house plants increase the colour and variety during the summer months.

Caring for the woodland garden

As mentioned earlier, a woodland garden will benefit from regular mulching. In winter or very early spring, cut down the dead stalks of perennials, thoroughly weed the garden and then cover with a feeding mulch of organic matter. It is neither practicable nor desirable to disturb the soil surface, in fact it is positively undesirable to do so. Whether you choose to remove dead stems or simply cut them into small pieces and leave them on the soil surface to further build up the organic layer is a matter of personal choice. The same is true with fallen leaves in the autumn. Removing them onto a compost heap does have the benefit of making any weeds easier to see and therefore easier to remove, but it also does means the need for returning that feeding mulch becomes more imperative.

As a general rule when planting into the native soil, the smaller the plants, the more weeding you will need to do. This is because the smaller plants do not cut out the light reaching the soil very efficiently and so opportunistic weeds seize the chance to grow. Among small plants the weeds do not need to grow very much before they smother the desired inhabitants. They can also be glaringly conspicuous in a low planting: a few 1-ft. (30-cm) weeds of virtually any kind will make a bed of small plants look untidy, whereas those same weeds in plantings of similar height or taller than the weeds would hardly be noticed. Beds filled with smaller bulbs and low alpines take as much time to weed as much larger areas filled with taller perennials. It is worth considering at the outset of making a woodland garden, or any garden for that matter, where a wide range of plants is anticipated, how the weeds are likely to respond to the plant mix.

Irrigation is not an easy subject for me to discuss. In my relatively wet climate I try not to water anything except for during the first few months after planting and then just to keep the newcomer alive until its roots can spread out. Obviously in climates where very little, if any, rain falls during the summer this is not an option and you may have to provide supplemental irrigation during the hottest and driest months. My only comment on this would be I think universal, in that if you have to water, it is better to give a good drenching infrequently than to give small amounts frequently, which attracts the feeding roots of plants to the surface where they will more quickly dry out. Mulching beds with organic materials of any kind will also help with water retention in the soil below.

Anatomy of a woodland border

Although every garden has different conditions, I believe almost any site can contain an area devoted to woodlanders. To demonstrate how it is possible to have a balanced all-encompassing approach to woodland planting I thought it might be useful to analyze a planting area I have made at Wildside which encapsulates many of the ideas discussed in the previous chapters. I created this garden in in a courtyard where there was previously no shade whatsoever.

The area is approximately 50 ft. long × 26 ft. wide (15 × 8 m), and runs along the north side of a substantial pergola which is covered with wisteria varieties. The pergola provides the principal shading and the walls provides shelter and further shade. The plantings are in raised beds that have been land formed to provide drainage and interest. Small widely spaced vertical shrubs supply colour and dappled shade, and the remainder is planted with a range of plants chosen to supply year-round form and colour.

In this cross section, the planting areas are all raised above the surrounding paths with the main bed landscaped into a series of gently undulating mounds. This helps to ensure the plants growing in them do not get waterlogged. There is an adobe-like wall built between the pergola posts all along the southern edge providing shelter and shade.

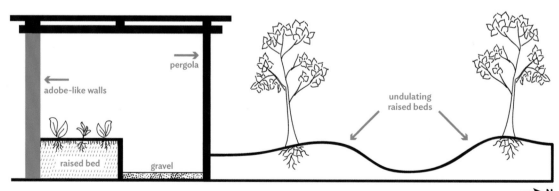

Winter

In the winter, shrubs (most of which are evergreen) help provide structure and interest, backing this up in the growing season with flowers of their own and providing shade for the lower-growing plants beneath. Most of the shrubs have an upright habit which maximizes the planting space around them. The exception are the viburnum and azaleas, which have arching rounded habits, but I was still able to plant underneath them as they are deciduous and I removed some of their lower branches without compromising their overall forms. Although all these shrubs are surprisingly hardy in this situation, coping with 5°F (−15°C) without succumbing, I chose them mainly for their form and flowering times.

Apart from the evergreens and the tracery and shape of the deciduous shrubs, the pergola itself, coloured adobe-like walls, the land forming, tree stumps and terracotta pot all help to furnish the winter appearance. Some of the planting choices in this woodland bed such as the yucca and the cordyline help to make the visual transition from shady bed to an adjacent bed, which is in full sun and filled many spikey and grassy foliage plants.

The raised bed under the pergola has the potential for growing special woodland treasures in conditions which are perfect for them away from the hurly-burly of a mixed border. An added advantage is that they are raised up to make weeding and closer inspection easier. An identical adjacent raised bed further along under the pergola has already been planted with woodland specials such as Chinese epimediums, corydalis, erythroniums in variety, double hellebores and trilliums.

Plant list

1. *Cordyline australis*
2. *Daphne* 'White Queen'
3. *Daphne ×burkwoodii* 'Albert Burkwood'
4. *Eucryphia lucida* 'Ballerina'
5. *Libertia* 'Amazing Grace'
6. *Lomatia ferrunginea*
7. *Magnolia grandiflora* 'Kay Parris'
8. *Magnolia laevifolia* 'Gail's Favourite'
9. *Rhododendron vaseyi* (azalea)
10. *Viburnum carlesii* 'Diane'
11. *Yucca flaccida* 'Golden Sword'
12. *Eucryphia moorei*

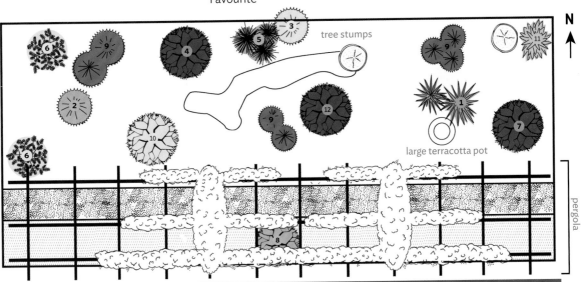

tree stumps

large terracotta pot

pergola

N

Spring

With the relatively mild winters at Wildside, spring can be a very long season, in some years stretching from mid-February through to mid-May, so it is unlikely that all of the plants shown in bloom on this plan will be out at the same time. In keeping with woodland gardens generally, however, this border has its main flowering in spring.

The principal components of this spring display are the hellebores. I prefer to loosely group the same colours together, so primrose yellow hellebores stretch from the top left of the plan through to the bottom right. The subsequent placings of the blue corydalis and primroses accentuate the colour of the hellebores. I would normally prefer to associate dark blue primroses with primrose-coloured ones, that yellow and blue combination being a very telling one, but in this case the drift of hellebores would overpower the more subtle primrose grouping, so I have opted for a more punchy and rather less natural combination of dark blue with the startling white of *Primula* 'Gigha'.

Around the edges of the bed, hellebores in the red–pink colour range combine early in spring with the scented pink viburnum flowers and the heavily fragrant white flowers of the *Magnolia ovalifolia*. These shrubs provide colour at head height beside the path which is where smaller plants meriting closer inspection are also planted, as well as other hellebores with intricate inner markings. A few weeks later the scentless but very beautiful *Rhododendron vaseyi*, planted at various points further into the border, provides the top colour. Raised from seed, this deciduous azalea shows subtle variations within its clean pale pink flowers, lending a natural feel to the bed. Over the next few years I'll add many more spring-flowering plants as gaps in the planting become apparent.

Rhododendron atlanticum is a deciduous scented azalea that could be used in place of *R. vaseyi* in a smaller garden.

Spring-blooming flowers

1. *Anemone ×lipsiensis* 'Pallida'
2. *Camassia leichtlinii* 'Treasure's Double'
3. *Corydalis flexuosa*
4. *Cypripedium reginae* with *Primula kisoana*
5. *Daphne* 'White Queen'
6. *Epimedium* 'Amber Queen'
7. *Helleborus ×hybridus*
8. *Libertia* 'Amazing Grace'
9. *Magnolia laevifolia* 'Gail's Favourite'
10. *Melittis melissophyllum*
11. *Primula* 'Ingram's Blue' and 'Gigha'
12. *Daphne ×burkwoodii*
13. *Rhododendron vaseyi*
14. *Trillium grandiflorum*
15. *Viburnum carlesii* 'Diane'

Wisteria on pergola in bloom

Summer

Verbena bonariensis, Stipa tenuissima and *Sedum telephium* hybrids have seeded themselves from sunnier parts of the garden in various places through the bed and all need to be thinned before they rapidly smother something more precious. As the shade levels increase when the surrounding trees and shrubs grow taller, these sun-lovers will gradually disappear.

The border in late summer is filled with the warm tones of dahlias and the spiky foliage of *Yucca flaccida* 'Golden Sword'.

In early summer the wisterias are in flower on the pergola, a highlight of any time of the year. I prune them to stay on the lines of the top timbers, allowing shafts of sunlight to penetrate to ground level. This is also when the Asiatic hybrid lilies flower. In the past I have avoided using these lilies, thinking them too stiff and solid for natural-looking plantings, but having tried them in this bed within the formal parameters of the courtyard I have turned into a convert. This after all, like many gardens, is not a natural setting even though the planting can have a naturalness to it, and I will use a lot more of these lilies in the coming years.

Early summer is also when the silver-leaved ferns, *Athyrium otophorum* var. *okanum*, should look their best, although they haven't performed as well here as I had hoped. It may be because I moved them from another part of the garden as mature plants and they haven't yet settled in yet, but after three years their time here is numbered unless they improve, to be replaced with the more silvery *Athyrium* 'Ghost'. Perhaps the most surprising element in this border are the dahlias. These are not plants I previously would have considered for a semi-shady border, but they work because they are late coming into growth and so are still below ground, or only just poking through, when all the smaller spring flowers are at their best. In another bed the emerging purple leaves of *Dahlia* 'Moonfire' look surprisingly good surrounded by the white-flowered *Trillium simile*. By the time the dahlias have grown to flowering size, so have other tall neighbours and they no longer seem incongruous. Their bright flowers light up these shady areas like beacons until the first frosts of autumn.

Joining the dahlias later in the summer comes the peerless *Thalictrum delavayi*. There are many newer thalictrum introductions but to me this long-established species is still one of the best. I discovered long ago it is a wonderful companion for low-growing woodland spring flowers, its emerging maidenhair-like foliage a perfect foil for them in flower and perfect shading for them as the thalictrum grows. I have used the variegated *Pelargonium* 'Vancouver Centennial' as a foil for the variegated yucca and the dahlias, but as the magnolia and yucca grow bigger there may not be room or sufficient light for it.

Summer-blooming flowers

1. *Athyrium otophorum* var. *okanum*
2. *Dahlia* 'Moonfire'
3. *Dahlia australis*
4. *Dahlia coccinea*
5. *Lilium*
6. *Lomatia ferruginea*
7. *Pelargonium* 'Vancouver Centennial'
8. *Roscoea* 'Wisley Amethyst'
9. *Thalictrum delavayi*
10. *Yucca flaccida* 'Golden Sword'
11. *Roscoea australis*

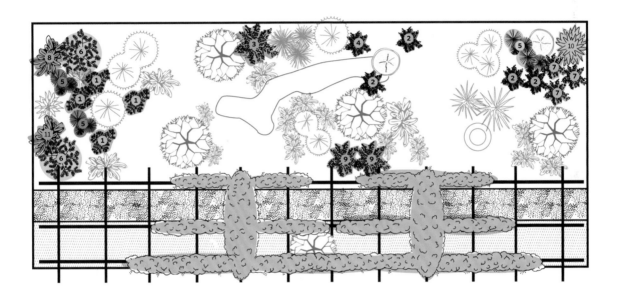

Early autumn

As the season moves from late summer into early autumn, flowers emerge in the plants that to this point have been contributing with their foliage and shape alone. The dahlias are still going strong but are now joined in flower by the eucryphias and *Chrysanthemum* 'Tapestry Rose', the latter flowering from early late summer through into midautumn. *Aster divaricatus* and *A. cordifolius* provide large patches of colour alongside the brilliant turquoise blue of *Salvia uliginosa* with self-seeding *Sedum telephium* hybrids popping up in unexpected places.

Roscoea 'Royal Purple', a new hybrid raised by Blackthorn Nursery, bears purple foliage on purple-red stems and reddish purple flowers.

One of the highlights of this time of year is provided by *Roscoea* 'Royal Purple', which forms a striking combination with the silver-leaved ferns planted nearby. This coming season I will plant more *Begonia evansiana* near this combination, as it too has a strong red-purple flush to the stems and leaves and graceful arching heads of soft pink flowers which should look good with the darker flowers of the roscoea. In a neighbouring bed I have purple-foliaged *Saxifraga fortunei* which also flowers in early autumn and I imagine its clouds of fluffy white flowers would also look good if planted nearby. Maybe *S. cuscutiformis* would also work well with this grouping, as it combines colour elements of both the roscoea and the athyrium, but I will need to find room for its spreading carpet of rounded leaves, red flushed on their underside and silver mottled above.

Whether in sun or shade, I use variations on this technique for combining plants throughout the garden. Repeating a factor which links different plants when planted together instils a subtle harmony to any combination. In this case it is the suggestion of a purplish red flush to foliage or stems, or a hint of silver colouration, but it might equally well be a link between foliage types or plant habit that is the unifying factor.

Autumn-blooming plants

1. *Aster cordifolius* hybrid
2. *Aster divaricatus*
3. *Athyrium otophorum* var. *okanum*
4. *Begonia evansiana* 'Alba'
5. *Chrysanthemum* 'Tapestry Rose'

6. *Dahlia* 'Moonfire'
7. *Dahlia australis*
8. *Dahlia coccinea*
9. *Eucryphia moorei*
10. *Magnolia grandiflora* 'Kay Parris'

11. *Pelargonium* 'Vancouver Centennial'
12. *Roscoea* 'Royal Purple'
13. *Salvia uliginosa*
14. *Eucryphia lucida* 'Ballerina'

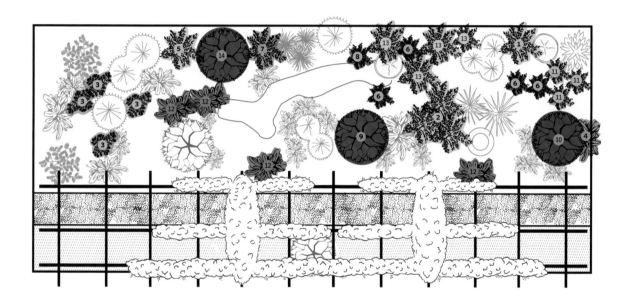

Geranium asphodeloides plays off 'Huntercombe Purple', 'Maggie Mott' and 'Moonlight' violas to great effect at the front of this shady border.

Plant Directory

Japanese maples are among my favourite garden trees, which with age develop sinous and striking trunks and branches.

Woodland Trees & Shrubs

There is such a wide range of plants that will grow in "woodland" conditions that many books on the subject quite reasonably steer clear of woody plants. But I include in this section shrubs or small trees that grow tall enough to produce sufficient shading in their own right for plants to grow below them. This selection represents the species and cultivars of genera I have used successfully in this capacity as understorey woody plants. The criteria required for their inclusion is that the tree or shrub must have at least two seasons of beauty, preferably more. This seasonal interest can result from flowers, colourful young growth, good summer foliage, autumn display, or trunk and branch colour. Also, and very important (although subjective), the plant must have a good habit that is sympathetic to its surroundings.

Virtually all the smaller woodland shrubs, as well as huge genera such as *Rhododendron* and *Hydrangea* (which have merited many books in their own right), have been excluded here. This is not an easy decision to make because these are wonderful shrubs perfectly suited to woodland conditions and I grow many of both at Wildside.

Acer
maple
Native to the northern hemisphere
Zones vary by species

The Japanese maples are probably my favourite woody plants. It was to this group of plants I turned first when dreaming of our new garden at Wildside, before I had even begun to form the mounds and banks on which to plant them. They combine grace of form and foliage with colourful, even spectacular, spring and fall displays. For year-round interest there can be few

Acer griseum

woody plants that match the qualities that their foliage in all its guises brings to the garden—as fine-fingered as the narrowest of grasses, as graceful as a ferns or as colourful as any flowering shrub.

Although there are many species of maple growing in Japan, the common name "Japanese maple" usually refers to varieties or hybrids between the species *Acer palmatum*, *A. shiraswanum* or *A. japonicum* (all hardy to zone 5). Such is the range in height, form and foliage that where climatic conditions allow there are a bewildering variety of Japanese maple cultivars to suit almost any position. As a general rule I would say the yellow-leaved varieties, those with thread-like divided leaves and those with thin-textured leaves are more likely to scorch in full sun, even in a wet climate, and are better given some shade.

Japanese maples are renowned for their autumn foliage but not all them are equally spectacular, so if fall colour is important to you be sure to research the plant before you commit to it. Some older named varieties such as 'Chishio', 'Corallinum' and 'Shindeshojo'—along with a host of other new ones—may in fact have very little fall interest, but have particularly bright emerging foliage of shrimp pink or red over

Acer palmatum var. dissectum 'Flavescens'

Assorted Acer palmatum var. dissectum

a long period in the spring. Combined with white or pastel pink evergreen azaleas which flower at the same time, they create eye-popping patches of colour.

Generally I prefer to use more of the types which colour up well in the fall. Some of these, such as the famed 'Osakazuki' (reliably fall-colouring scarlet), have very limited appeal at leaf emergence other than their general fresh green-ness, but there are others whose young leaves emerge in various shades of bronze to purple-red, gradually fading to green over a period of several weeks. Examples include 'Autumn Glory', 'Chitoseyama' and 'Matsukase', along with many purple-leaved varieties which are equally good during both seasons.

Over the winter months, the bark and twig colour of Japanese maples add interest even after the leaves have fallen, and their graceful outlines become breathtakingly beautiful silhouetted against a backdrop of snow. With heavy dews and after rainfall, the thin twig structure holds water droplets which catch the light and sparkle in the low morning sunshine of an early winter morning like a myriad diamonds—one of the magical visual highlights of the whole year.

Perhaps the most spectacular of Japanese maples for bark effect is *Acer palmatum* 'Sango-kaku' which many of us know better as *A. palmatum* 'Senkaki'. This is the coral bark maple whose branches and twigs

Acer palmatum 'Osakazuki'

are bright coral-red. Seen at a distance in winter sunlight against a dark background, this plant glows as if in bloom. By chance I planted several of these near my witch hazels against just such a distant dark wood and their similarity to *Hamamelis* 'Diane' makes it appear as if they are all in flower together. Unlike the witch hazels, however, the winter effect of the maple lasts all winter. In addition to the eye-catching bark, the autumn colour of 'Sango-kaku' lasts longer than any other plant I know (clear yellow for at least three or four weeks). *Liquidambar styraciflua* 'Worplesden' which turns shades of purple, red and yellow is the only other tree to rival it for a long fall colour display.

The Chinese species *Acer griseum* (zone 4)

has a fair claim to being one of the finest of all small trees. Its common name of paper-bark maple refers to its cinnamon-coloured peeling bark. The fingered trifoliate leaves, reminiscent of Japanese maples, turn wonderful shades of orange and red in the autumn. When planted where the lowering sun can shine through the curls and ringlets of its bark, this tree is just as beautiful when dormant. I have planted twelve of these in closely scattered groups near the entrance to our garden and underplanted them with clumps of widely spaced evergreen azaleas and dwarf rhododendrons. With spring bulbs to fill the gaps in between the trees, the result is a year-round structural and textural combination which fills me with excited anticipation for the future.

Cold, wet "feet" are anathema to maples, so I have planted them at Wildside in moisture-retentive soil on raised banks to give them the drainage they need to thrive. If given these conditions, all but the finely dissected varieties are surprisingly tolerant of the wind.

Cercidiphyllum japonicum
Japanese katsura tree
Native to Japan and China
Zone 4

Japanese katsura tree is another personal favourite. I remember as a child visiting Westonbirt Arboretum in Gloucestershire, where 50-ft. (15-m) specimens turn clear yellow in autumn. I take pleasure from this species at all stages of its life, from sapling to mature tree, from single specimen to a copse of them. The dainty oval leaves are a delight from first opening in the spring until their spectacular fall in autumn, when the smell of caramelized sugar from the falling leaves is particularly potent. The habit of the tree is always graceful, generally upright but arching. I have even seen in Sweden a small forestry plantation of katsura trees, their graceful tall slim trunks

looking more Lothlorien-like than would seem possible.

Commercially, Japanese katsura is widely available and because it is raised from seed there is variation among specimens. I find that those showing more purple in their emerging leaves will colour up more spectacularly in the autumn. The best forms I have grown turn clear yellow towards the centre of the tree, with brilliant oranges and scarlets on the leaves exposed to more light.

I know of two taller varieties, both good and both completely different. *Cercidiphyllum japonicum* forma *pendulum* needs space to really show off its arching, then pendulous branches. I loved its habit but the specimen I grew lacked colourful emerging leaves and was disappointing in the fall. *Cercidiphyllum japonicum* 'Rotfuchs' by contrast is strongly columnar in its youth before starting to spread its branches in middle age. Its most striking feature though is its purple foliage, a rich purple-red in the spring turning to greyish purple by midsummer, but this variety too refuses to show much in the way of fall colour. For much smaller planting schemes there is the slower-growing variety 'Boyd's Dwarf' reaching only about 6 ft. (2 m) at maturity. 'Heronswood Globe' grows taller maturing at about 20 ft. (6 m). None of these seem particularly fussy regarding soils or aspect, but their thin-textured foliage does appear susceptible to windy sites particularly as they leaf out so early in the spring.

Cornus
dogwood
Native to North American and eastern Asia
Zones vary by species

The flowering dogwoods are another classic small tree for the edge of the woodland, thriving in part shade or in full sun. The native North American flowering dogwoods, *Cornus florida* (zone 5) and *C. nuttalli* (zone 7), do well in the sunnier southern counties of the United Kingdom (generally not flowering so well in the wetter west) but the former does spectacularly well in areas with drier, hotter summers in the United States and Canada. Although to date I have had no experience of it, *Cornus florida* varieties particularly are susceptible to the fungal disease anthracnose, so check to see if the disease is prevalent in your area before planting. Hybrids between these two species and the Chinese dogwood, *C. kousa* (zone 5), are more suited to a wider climatic area as the latter species is freer flowering and even happier in wetter climes. *Cornus kousa* demands an acid soil but its Chinese counterpart *C. kousa* var. *chinensis* is more tolerant of alkaline soils.

Both *Cornus kousa* and *C. kousa* var. *chinensis* can produce wonderful four-petalled flowers (really bracts) that crowd the tops of the branches in early summer, followed by a significant display of pinkish red strawberry-like fruits. Good orange-red fall colour and a generally tiered habit make for a first-class small tree or large shrub. I particularly like the Chinese dogwood variety 'Satomi'. It has that very good autumn colour and the bracts open pink and darken to a glowing red with age, although the colour may not be as intense in areas where dry summers are the norm.

I have said I am not a great fan of variegated plants, but some of my favourite large shrubs and small trees are in fact dogwoods with this feature. As a lad I remember going to the Bath Botanic Garden and being completely entranced by a pair of magnificent *Cornus controversa* 'Variegata' (zone 5) commonly known as the wedding cake tree. I have enjoyed its presence in my garden for thirty-five years, and remain captivated by it when looking up as the summer sun streams through its layered branches of silvery white leaves edged and flushed with maroon on ruby twigs. The variety *C. controversa* 'Marginata Nord' has

Cornus florida 'Rubra'

Cornus florida 'Cherokee Chief'

Corylopsis platypetala

a slightly greyer cast to its foliage, appears to be shorter and more wide spreading, and flowers freely with umbels of fluffy white flowers in early summer all along the top of the branches. I am presently growing a golden-leaved wedding cake tree, 'Golden Wedding', which sounds enticing but so far I'm struggling to get it established and it is too young to make any assessments.

Other silver-leaved *Cornus* include *C. alternifolia* 'Argentea' (zone 4), which has a similar tiered habit, but with smaller leaves. It is quite slow growing, with a suggested eventual height of 6 ft. (2 m) but I have seen it in exceptional circumstances reaching over three times this height. Producing an equally clean-cut variegation to *C. controversa* 'Variegata' is a variegated Chinese dogwood, *C. kousa* var. *chinensis* 'Wolfeyes'. The habit and foliage of this plant is similar to the wedding cake tree and it has the added advantage of white flowers in summer and good colour in autumn, when the white sections of the leaves turn pinkish purple.

In a more naturalistic setting I prefer to stick with the green-leaved varieties and species. *Cornus nuttalli* itself is not a good garden plant in the United Kingdom as it seems to need the warmer, drier summers of its Pacific Northwest home, but its hybrids with *C. kousa* and *C. florida* have produced some excellent garden plants. *Cornus* 'Norman Hadden' (zone 6) was one of the first in the United Kingdom and is

still good. *Cornus* 'Eddie's White Wonder' (zone 7) makes a large rounded shrub reaching about 16 ft. (5 m) high and covered in midspring with large white flowers more akin to its *C. nuttalli* parent. I have planted small groves of them at Wildside which make quite a feature at that time of year. The newer hybrid called 'Venus' appears to be similar but even more vigorous and free flowering. In truth, there are now so many flowering dogwood varieties, if I had space I would probably attempt to grow them all.

Corylopsis

winter hazel
Native to the eastern Himalayas
Zones vary by species

Sadly somewhat neglected by gardeners, these shrubs are stalwarts of the woodland spring garden. They bear some resemblances to hazel, *Corylus avellana*, in flower, foliage and bark but are more refined and colourful on each count. All have good yellow autumn colour and their early spring flowers borne in dangling racemes are in a few cases deliciously scented. With the exception of *Corylopsis pauciflora* I would not consider them to be specimen plants, being best as background shrubs or in mixed plantings, such as at Winterthur in Delaware, where in early spring they dance a fabulous pas de deux in purplish blue and primrose-yellow with *Rhododendron david-sonianum* and *R. augustinii.*

Some such as *Corylopsis willmottiae* (zone 6) are 10–13 ft. (3–4 m) high, upright shrubs that arch slightly with age; *C. sinensis* (zone 6) and *C. gotoana* (zone 5) generally are much more spreading but slightly shorter, with *C. platypetala* (zone 7) somewhat between the two types in habit. The sole lower-growing corylopsis is *C. pauciflora* (zone 6), which forms a domed, twiggy spreading shrub, beautiful through-out the winter months, approximately 3 ft. (1 m) high, although ancient unpruned specimens may be double that. The massed racemes of scented primrose-yellow flow-ers crowding the branches are followed by purple-flushed young foliage which turns a rich orange-yellow in the fall, altogether a classy plant for a semi-shaded spot. Given a reasonable depth of any soil they are all easily grown, except for *C. pauciflora*, which needs an acid soil.

Daphne

**Native (those mentioned)
  to the Himalayas
Zone 7**

Some of my favourite evergreen shrubs for the woodland edge are varieties or hybrids of *Daphne bholua, D. sureil* and *D. acutiloba*. This group of daphnes is not completely hardy, suffering leafdrop at around 5°F (−15°C) and likely extinction at temperatures below 1°F (−17°C). They are, however, magnificent and mostly highly scented shrubs that flower in winter and very early spring.

The natural species variation within *Daphne bholua* means there are selections that will bloom with us from early winter through to very early spring. The earliest is 'Darjeeling', usually at its best before Christmas and as with all the bholuas very highly scented. At Wildside it grows about 6 ft. (2 m) high, upright but twiggy.

Daphne bholua 'Alba'

In midwinter the next group of cultivars start to bloom and these include the largest-growing stars of the whole genus, 'Jacqueline Postill' and 'Gurkha'. These are also the hardiest of the group, naturally dropping their leaves without harm if the temperatures drop below their comfort zone but still succumbing if it gets even colder. If grown on their own roots they can sucker and produce a thicket of upright stems typically up to about 10 ft. (3 m) high. Both have relatively large flowers which mass on the smaller twigs and turn the bushes into columns of pale laven-der, flooding the whole area with heavy perfume. *Daphne bholua* 'Peter Smithers' flowers around the same time but is darker in flower. The pure white-flowered 'Alba' flowers early in the winter and does appear to be a little less hardy than the others but has a particularly delicious scent. Grown under cover they will all flower earlier than when grown outside and are likely to set some seed. I have raised seedlings from these, and although they are not true to type I have planted them out on banks in the hopes they will form some copses of mixed bholua daphnes which I will undercarpet with massed early spring flowers and bulbs.

Hybrids include *Daphne* 'Spring Herald' (*D. bholua* × *D. acutiloba*) and *D.* 'Spring Beauty' (*D. bholua* × *D. sureil*). 'Spring Herald', with its *D. acutiloba* 'Fragrant Cloud' parentage, flowers in midspring and escapes some of the vagaries of early spring weather (not really an issue for the plant but certainly making it more pleasurable for the gardener who wants to enjoy them). It too, if grown on its own roots, will sucker gently making a plant about 6 ft. (2 m) high. 'Spring Beauty' makes an upright plant of similar shape but has shown no sign of suckering to date. Its flowers are not as heavily scented, are pink in colour and have a very refined form, a characteristic inherited from its *D. sureil* parent.

Eucryphia ×*intermedia* 'Rostrevor'

The vast majority of daphnes are sun-lovers, but the bholua group are naturally edge-of-woodland plants. As with all daphnes, good drainage is essential, but given this, those mentioned are happy in any good soil in a site sheltered from strong winds.

Eucryphia
Temperate areas of South America and Australasia
Zone 8

With the exception of *Eucryphia glutinosa*, these are evergreen, upright, white-flowered small trees for cooler climates where winter temperatures are unlikely to drop below −4°F (−20°C) for extended periods. In a woodland garden they can fill the role that holly occupies in northern European woods by helping to filter the wind and providing evergreen screening. In a climate as wet as mine, they can be specimen trees in full sun, providing dappled shade below and high level flowers in late summer. Most eucryphias prefer acid soils but I have grown nearly all the evergreen ones in slightly alkaline conditions in the past.

I use all the evergreen eucryphias extensively and choosing between them is not easy. However, among the taller growing ones I would not be without *Eucryphia moorei* and *E.* ×*intermedia* 'Rostrevor'. (*Eucryphia* 'Rostrevor' is the name given to the clone of *E.* ×*intermedia* usually available in the United Kingdom.) It has glossy dark green leaves and masses of large white-scented flowers in late summer and early autumn. I have found it to be surprisingly tolerant of windy sites. *Eucryphia moorei* is not supposed to be hardy but it has shown little damage during several winters when temperatures reached 5°F (−15°C). It has a columnar habit, pinnate greyish green foliage and in midautumn the whole shrub is completely covered in 1-in.-wide (2 cm), honey-scented flowers.

Eucryphia lucida hails from Tasmania and is usually grown as an upright shrub about 10 ft. (3 m) high. Keen-eyed local plantsman Ken Gillanders found some variegated forms and two pink-flowered forms, which he named 'Pink Cloud' and 'Ballerina'. 'Ballerina' is the best with more red in the flower centre and strongly pink picotee edges to the petals. This is such a striking plant that when it blooms in late summer, requests for its name outstrip all other enquiries from visitors to Wildside.

The one deciduous eucryphia (actually evergreen in its native Chile) is *Eucryphia glutinosa*, a beautiful, slow-growing, densely twiggy shrub with upright growth. The handsome pinnate foliage turns orange-red in autumn, but although the fall colour is impressive, it is truly memorable for its late-summer mass of large, white, bowl-shaped flowers with their prominent boss of yellow-anthered stamens. *Eucryphia glutinosa* needs an acid soil but is perfectly hardy. Like most eucryphias it does not flower well until it reaches about 6 ft. (2 m) in height.

Hamamelis
witch hazel
Native to eastern Asia
Zone 5

The witch hazels are another classic winter- and early-spring-flowering group for woodland edges and glades. Almost impervious to cold weather, their habit, foliage and branch structure is so reminiscent of the native British hazel, *Corylus avellana*, they blend seamlessly with the countryside that surrounds us. I would love to grow more than I do but have to restrict myself.

My favourite witch hazel has long been *Hamamelis ×intermedia* 'Pallida' with its strongly scented, bright yellow flowers starting usually with us sometime midwinter and continuing for four to

Hamamelis ×intermedia varieties (from front) 'Ruby Glow', 'Orange Beauty' and 'Pallida'

six weeks. The clear orange-yellow fall foliage colour is as good as any other fall shrub. *Hamamelis* 'Moonlight' is paler in flower, free-flowering, not quite as strongly scented but has the unfortunate habit, at least in its youth and in my garden, of hanging onto its dead leaves which compromises its otherwise excellent flowering display. *Hamamelis mollis*, Chinese witch hazel, flowers earlier with smaller blooms and to my nose is not as strongly scented. *Hamamelis mollis* 'Harry' is a version of the species that flowers freely with more-orange blooms with a strong, fresh fragrance. Among the real orange-flowered cultivars, *H.* 'Aphrodite' is a similar colour but with larger flowers than the older *H. ×intermedia* 'Jelena' (whose foliage turns a good orange-red in fall) but it has reputedly a stronger scent which has to date eluded me. The only red-flowered variety I grow is *H.* 'Diane' which usually flowers a month later than 'Pallida' and shows good orange-red fall colour as well.

Magnolia
Native to eastern Asia and garden origin
Zones vary by species

Magnolias form a major component of my woodland plantings and I have 100 or so planted at Wildside. Their flowers are a perfect complement for the carpet of spring-flowering woodland plants that can be grown beneath them. Almost as important to me though are the colour and form of the magnolia trunks, which in clean air, away from car pollution, develop wonderful lichen growths on their silvered bark. I often plant several magnolias in close proximity so their multiple trunks provide a sculptural element to what would otherwise be a mass of surrounding vegetation, an idea that first came to me when a nurseryman friend offered me some past-their-best *Magnolia ×soulangeana* (zone 5). I planted them quite close together, reasoning that even if most died there would still be one or two left. In the event the individual plants and trunks grew at different speeds, and over the years resulted in a very natural-looking copse. Knowing that magnolias have dense root systems which dislike being disturbed I planted spring bulbs between them when the trees were very young and then just left them to seed and spread around of their own accord.

The concept worked so well that I repeated the idea with the smaller-growing *Magnolia stellata* (zone 4). This has worked out even better as the natural form of the species is to hold its branches and flowers nearer the ground and so closer to the woodland flowers planted beneath, creating a more impressive and eye-catching display. With taller magnolias such as *M. ×loebneri* 'Merrill' (zone 5) or *M. ×proctoriana* (zone 5) the underplanting has been of a combination of lower-growing shrubs like *Corylopsis pauciflora* and evergreen azaleas, with spring ephemerals growing beneath these shrubs. I have even

Magnolia ×loebneri 'Merrill'

Growing in any good soil they do best on neutral or acid formations. Young plants can have an occasional tendency to grow more sideways than up and so some gardeners train up a leading shoot to gain height. Personally, if I know the variety at maturity has the broad vase shape typical of the species I am content to let the plant choose its own time to grow upwards. They are sufficiently slow-growing that I am very reluctant to prune witch hazels anyway, other than to remove small crossing branches or sprigs when in flower to appreciate the beautiful scent indoors.

Michelia yunnanensis (Magnolia laevifolia)

attempted this multiple group method with one of my favourite magnolias, the tall-growing Asiatic species *M. sprengeri* 'Diva' (zone 5). Unusually for one of the tree-like Asiatics, the large rose-pink-flushed flowers on this species are so gloriously scented that I suspect my version of heaven would smell like this. A mature specimen can cast its fragrance for at least 100 yards downwind, an annual highlight for eye and nose.

Michelia yunnanensis
Native to China
Zone 8

The tree that came to me as *Michelia yunnanensis* is probably, at least for the time being, now grouped under *Magnolia* as *Magnolia laevifolia*. It is an evergreen species with small, leathery leaves (for a magnolia) and a long succession of highly scented white flowers in the leaf axils in spring. My reference books suggest this plant is not at all hardy but it has withstood with no damage at all through several winters where the temperature has infrequently dropped to 5°F (−15°C). Even in a spring where we experienced gale-force winds close to freezing for nearly a month, this plant, although defoliated, made a full recovery the following summer. An open, freely branching upright habit and not overpowering foliage makes it an ideal candidate for creating a living screen and providing shade in a sheltered site. The variety 'Gail's Favourite' has larger flowers and slightly larger leaves. It is more striking in flower but as a young plant at least does not appear to have the grace of habit of the species and only time will tell if it is quite as hardy.

I am making a steeply sloping bank

Stewartia pseudocamellia

Stewartia
Native to eastern Asia
Zone 4

Devotees of this genus rightly sing its praises but I feel it should come with a proviso. Although there is no doubt that mature stewartias are all they are cracked up to be, younger specimens often leave me feeling slightly underwhelmed. This is because some of their prime attributes, like their graceful upright habit, colourful marbled trunks and even full flowering potential, are not fully realized until maturity. It may be heretical to say so but even a specimen in full flower is unlikely to stop traffic, although it might when in spectacular fall colour. Having said all that, stewartias are lovely plants to live with all year round when they do reach that later stage. The species are all superficially similar with white dog rose–like flowers, beautiful autumn colour, lovely trunks and good upright habit. *Stewartia malacodendron* is the star flowering species, with its boss of purple stamens if that is the main draw for you, but is reputedly a bit less hardy and trickier to please. It grew well for me in my last garden but hadn't flowered after eight years from planting when I left, which perhaps only emphasizes my dilemma with the genus, that they are not plants for the impatient.

Styrax
snowbells, snowdrop tree
Native to China and Japan
Zone 5

Even though they don't have the year-round charms of stewartias, any styrax in full flower will in fact stop traffic. Sometimes called snowbells or the snowdrop tree (a common name also applied to halesias), a styrax in full bloom with a multitude of pendulous white flowers certainly lives up to its common name.

where I can grow a grove of michelia among a few taller-growing silver birch that provide high-level light shade. Along with the michelia will be widely spaced upright evergreens, such as *Daphne bholua* and *Eucryphia moorei*, with the deciduous, small-leaved and gracefully upright *Hoheria angustifolia* 'Borde Hill'. The lower branches on the michelia will be removed and together the smaller trees and shrubs will create a canopy that flowers for much of the year, all undercarpeted with spring-flowering woodland perennials.

Styrax japonica 'Pink Chimes'

Most species make small trees that eventually reach 20 ft. (6 m) high, the branches spreading with age. *Styrax japonica* is the slowest growing, more usually a large bush than tree, but a magnificent sight when the pure white, slightly scented flowers mass the underside of the branches in midsummer. There is a pink variety 'Beni-bana' ('Pink Chimes' is very similar) whose branches are semi-drooping, but surprisingly when I have raised seedlings from this variety at least half the ensuing progeny were virtually pendulous and nearly all had white flowers. These offspring made dome-shaped bushes about 6 ft. (2 m) high and are more reminiscent of a dissectum Japanese maple in habit. There are now named pink

and white pendulous forms of this species so perhaps someone else also made the same discovery. Slightly more treelike and vigorous, and widely vase shaped, is *S. formosana*. The white flowers may also be slightly bigger as well as more strongly scented. Both species have birch-like leaves that turn pale yellow in autumn.

Altogether different with more hazel-like foliage are another two species very similar to each other, *Styrax hemsleyana* and *S. obassia*. Both make small trees about 25 ft. (8 m) high, with widely spaced branches on a broadly vase-shaped habit. The white flowers in drooping panicles are sweetly scented, and the bolder foliage works very well in association with hydrangeas.

Aquilegia 'Double Red', *Geranium pratense* and *Euphorbia characias*

Woodland Perennials

If trees and tall shrubs form the structural framework for woodland gardens, then lower-growing shrubs and perennials represent the floors and furnishings. This blanket of cover at and below eye level produces the ever-changing kaleidoscope of colour and interest that makes woodland gardens so fascinating. An extensive overhead canopy results in a primary flowering period in the spring when more light is able to penetrate through the leafless trees. The more sunlight that reaches the plants, the longer the spring flowering season will last, after which the majority of summer interest will be provided by plants that continue to offer form and foliage. There is nothing better than perennials to offer that seasonal diversity.

As a general rule, the spring-flowering plants in this directory are suitable for a shady site—provided the shade is cast by deciduous trees. But the shade tolerance of perennials that flower in summer is much more dependent on the degree of shading. There is no set formula here but clues that might suggest any particular plant would benefit from more sunlight might be poor flowering, paler colouring of flowers or foliage than expected and straggly, leaning growth taller than available literature suggested. Some genera that straddle the categories of "perennial" and "bulb" are also included here, for example anemone and corydalis, some of whose members have tuberous roots (normally included under bulbs) while others have "normal" root systems with no swollen sections.

Actaea dahurica

Actaea

bugbane, baneberry
Native to North America and eastern Asia
Zone 6
Growth habit Group 7, Tall, clumping

Formerly and still considered as *Cimicifuga* by some experts, the bugbanes are medium to tall perennials best grown in good soil in part shade. Most flower towards the autumn with white flowers in bottlebrush-like narrow spikes held well above the arching clumps of variously divided foliage. These provide a structural contrast to the general sameness of other late-summer flowers and a link to the grasses which are also so prominent at this time of year.

The earliest to flower in midsummer is *Actaea simplex*, most commonly available in many purple-leaved forms. Some of these have white flowers; others are pink and held well above the leaves in the typical spikes, and many have now been selected for their dark stems and purple, almost black, foliage. All are worth growing but whether they come within the remit of this book is slightly dubious. They will certainly grow well in the dappled shade afforded by the woodland but the foliage colour will undoubtedly be much stronger with higher light levels. Somewhat later in the summer is the season for *A. cordifolia*, whose foliage resembles a particularly vigorous Japanese anemone. The flower spikes are very narrow with the flowers rather more yellow, but their dark stems add up to a plant of refined charm.

Very early autumn brings us to the flowering time of *Actaea dahurica*. This is the most showy of the actaeas, with widely branched spikes of white flowers on a plant 6 ft. (2 m) high. *Actaea matsumerae* blooms along with Michaelmas daisies in early autumn and the widely available 'White Pearl' reaches 6 ft. (2 m) in height with fresh green leaves all summer. I prefer the less vigorous 'Elstead variety' with its faintly purple-flushed foliage and dark purple stems accentuating the whiteness of the flowers.

Anemone
wood anemone, Japanese anemone
Native mostly to temperate regions
    of the northern hemisphere
Zones vary by species
Growth habit varies with species

Some of the most important anemones for the woodland behave as bulbs, appearing in early spring, flowering and then retreating below ground until the following year. The European wood anemone, *Anemone nemorosa* (zone 5), is one of these. Given cool conditions it will tolerate a wide variety of sites and can be grown among the roots of late-emerging hostas and rodgersias. I have taken this plant for granted as a guaranteed spring flower for reliability and tolerance, but increasingly I believe that wood anemones repay good husbandry. The best displays I have ever seen were in Ernie and Marietta O'Byrne's garden near Eugene in Oregon where they cover all their woodland beds with a deep, loose annual mulch. I now spread a thin layer of well-composted farmyard manure in late winter over the ground where anemones are planted and the result is much larger flowers.

There are many varieties of *Anemone nemorosa*, but were I to limit myself to just a few then 'Robinsoniana', with its large lavender-blue, greyish silver-backed flowers, would probably top the list. Of similar colour but flowering much later is 'Buckland' which has perhaps the largest flowers of any with the added advantage of being sweetly scented (a trait which only a few wood anemones share). Among the darker blues, 'Royal Blue' would be my choice for

Aster cordifolius with *Anemone hupehensis* 'Bowles Pink'

Anemone nemorosa

Anemone blanda var. *scynthinica* and chionodoxas

creating a patch of colour in the garden, but for an up-close-and-personal spot in this colour 'Miss Eunice' is worth searching for. She has flowers of beautiful form reminiscent of a good hepatica. Among the taller single whites there is not much to choose between 'Lady Doneraile', 'Leeds Variety' and 'Lychette'. 'Polar Star' would be a good choice for a low-growing white anemone. There are various pink forms, most of which start white and darken to various shades but none of the commercially available ones are a good clean pink from the start. Of the doubles, I would limit myself to just one, the beautiful 'Vestal', a fully double white whose flowers last longer than all the singles and reliably covers itself in flower. To my eye the numerous novelty varieties have somewhat malformed flowers.

Of very similar habit but with bright yellow flowers is *Anemone ranunculoides* (zone 4). It is pretty and spreads quite quickly when happy but it doesn't make the same visual impact as *A. nemorosa*. A

hybrid of the two species is *A. ×lipsien-sis* (zone 4) which in the form 'Pallida' is a beautiful lemon-yellow with purple-flushed young leaves, a fabulous if fleeting combination.

A visit to Scottish gardens many years ago left an indelible memory of *Anemone obtusiloba* (zone 5) in both its blue and white forms. This makes compact clumps of foliage 6–8 in. (15–20 cm) high topped by 2-in. (5-cm) single flowers like wood anemones. It was the star plant of that late spring visit, but attempts to grow the species in my own garden always resulted in disappointment with flowers only a third of that size. The general consensus within the gardening fraternity at the time was this was the result of the cooler Scottish growing conditions, but recently a clone has been distributed which is producing those large flowers further south and breeding true from seed. I have just acquired the plant again and am hoping for better luck. There is a yellow, blue-backed flower form of this species, 'Sulphurea', but mine has so far only produced the same small flowers. Nonetheless, I am happy to have it as a little treasure to admire at close quarters.

Much easier to grow in the garden is *Anemone rivularis* (zone 6) which will self-seed gently in cool, half-shady spots. This grows 24–30 in. (60–75 cm) high, with branching sprays of single, white, blue-backed flowers in early summer. It adds an

Anemone blanda and *Narcissus pseudonarcissus*

air of sophisticated wildness to any border. Of similar branching habit, flower colour and size is *A.* ×*leveillei* (zone 6) but it has slightly larger flowers with more petals and is slightly less wild looking.

Midway in size between these last two and *Anemone obtusiloba* is a new plant to me, *A.* 'Wild Swan' (zone 5). I first heard of this anemone some years ago when the celebrated plantsman Roy Lancaster came back from a trip to Elizabeth MacGregor's Scottish nursery absolutely full of a new plant he had seen there. Seeing it now I can understand his excitement. Growing 18–24 in. (45–60 cm) high, it is like a version on steroids of a cross between *A. rupicola* (a large-flowered but tricky woodlander) and one of the flowering Japanese anemones (*A.* ×*hybrida* or *A. hupehensis*) with extra-large white flowers—up to 4 in. (10 cm) across—with blue reverses. If deadheaded, it flowers for much of the summer and into fall. It could become a classic.

The ubiquitous autumn-flowering Japanese anemones are well entrenched in many gardens. There are legions of them, some almost too vigorous, but if you have the space they blend beautifully with Michaelmas daisies. If your planting style is more naturalistic, they can be put at the edge of the woodland, but be warned that they will only really happily co-exist with equally boisterous neighbours. I do love them though.

Anemonopsis macrophylla
Native to Japan
Zone 4
Growth habit Group 7, Tall, clumping

Anemonopsis macrophylla is a Japanese plant of quiet, elegant charm (a phrase beloved of nursery catalogues to denote a plant hardly worth growing, but this isn't a catalogue and I'm only promoting worthwhile plants). It is a refined perennial with attractive ferny foliage over which branching dark stems carry many lavender-mauve flowers. These hang demurely, hiding the intricacy of their inner structure, and close up they are very beautiful. Growing about 30 in. (75 cm) high, this plant needs shade and protection from the wind, otherwise it will scorch. I have recently acquired the pure white-flowered form 'White Queen'.

Asteranthera ovata

Asteranthera ovata
Native to Chile and Argentina
Zone 7
Growth habit Group 3, Tightly
   clumping evergreen

This creeping evergreen is for cool, moist acidic soils in partial shade. Given these conditions it can press itself against boulders, tree stumps and even climb gently up tree trunks or walls to a height of 13 ft. (4 m) where suited. I have found it loves hugging the surface of moistened peat blocks, rooting from the leaf axils as it grows.

Plant this at the base of its intended host as it seems reluctant to grow downwards. The very large red flowers (for the size of the plant) are produced from midsummer onwards. They are spectacular, and a sight not easily forgotten once seen.

Begonia
Native to eastern Asia
Zones vary by species
Growth habit Group 2, Low, clumping,
   and Group 6, Bold foliage plants

In cool, shady spots, begonias can provide some very valuable late-summer foliage contrasts at a time when those stalwarts of earlier in the year, the hostas, are beginning to look tired. In recent years there are many more species and foliage forms being introduced but none, to my knowledge, are reliably hardy. Many are borderline and some like *Begonia grandis* ssp. *evansiana* (zone 6) have withstood 5°F (−15°C) unprotected in our garden. Because it is so late to emerge, every year I wonder whether the winter has finally finished it off and, if it hasn't, whether I will plant it again. When

Begonia 'Metallic Mist' and *Plectranthus*

midautumn arrives I am amazed I ever doubted it, as the bronze-backed leaves look fresh and the arching sprays of flowers in either the white or pink forms begin to elongate. Both forms look great with late-flowering purple-leaved roscoeas and the dark foliage of dahlias. I leave the begonias and the dahlia tubers in the ground over winter and cover them with a thick mulch which helps them to survive.

Some of the beautiful silver- and purple-marbled begonias, like *Bergenia* 'Metallic Mist' and *B.* 'Beni tochiba', I do lift and bring in for the winter, even though they are meant to be hardy. The latter has foliage like a small household rex begonia, so I feel they are worth the effort, especially when they give months of beautiful contrast in a shady spot to the silver-leaved athyrium ferns.

Bergenia
elephant's ears
Native to central Asia to the Himalayas
Zones vary by species
Growth habit Group 6, Bold foliage plants

In drier soils bergenias can be very useful as bold foliage plants, especially as many are evergreen. In some ways, with their large, rounded glossy leaves, they fill the role that hostas do in more moisture-retentive soils. Their flowers too, in shades from near red through to white, are undeniably eye catching, but I still haven't been able to love them—partly because they are evergreen, and whenever I have grown them they tend to look too untidy throughout the year by holding on to far too many of their old leaves. Perhaps the secret of all those pictures I have seen of bergenias looking fabulous all winter is that very diligent gardeners remove these unsightly leaves, or maybe it is because the plants do not like my wet climate. As a result, I haven't grown many of the numerous hybrids available.

There are, however, bergenias I like a lot. *Bergenia emeiensis* (zone 6), for example, forms a compact evergreen clump with the large glossy leaves typical of the genus. The leaves lie almost flat and even in midwinter they are still fresh green and unblemished.

Bergenia 'Pink Ice'

The white flowers come very early in the spring and are held in very graceful sprays. If the plant has a fault it is this early flowering because the flowers can be hit by late frosts.

A hybrid of this species crossed with a white hybrid, raised by Robin White of Blackthorn Nursery, is *Bergenia* 'Pink Ice' (zone 6). It has all the attributes of the species but blooms later in spring with elegant sprays of open flowers tinged clear pink fading to white. It is beautiful in every sense.

I'm also fond of *Bergenia purpurascens* 'Irish Crimson' (zone 4), which has relatively small upstanding foliage of intense dark-reddish purple through the winter months. In spring, it produces deeper purple nodding flowers on tall elegant stems. It continues to hold on to some of its older leaves through the summer but not to such an extent that is beyond me to keep it looking tidy.

Campanula
bellflower
Native to temperate regions of the northern hemisphere
Zones vary by species
Growth habit Group 4, Prostrate, and Group 7, Tall, clumping

Most campanulas are sun lovers and I don't think I have deliberately ever planted one in the shade, but a few of the taller perennial species have seeded into shady niches in my garden and seem at home. It had never occurred to me that woodland might be the natural habitat for some campanulas, but in fact it is. In particular, the tall upright *Campanula latifolia* (zone 4) is from the woods of Europe and Asia. It forms a stiffly upright plant to 5 ft. (1.5 m) high, the top half of which is adorned with large bell-shaped flowers in midsummer.

Campanula lactiflora with astrantias and filipendulas

Typically these flowers are various shades of violet-blue but there is a pure white form, *C. latifolia* var. *alba*. There are also several named forms with flowers that have dark purple centres: 'Gloaming' has pale lilac flowers with these darker centres, and 'Buckland' has white flowers with purple centres; it was raised at the Garden House but 'Faichem Lilac' from a Scottish garden appears to be similar.

Campanula persicifolia (zone 3) is also found in woodlands from the Balkans through to North Africa. It is shorter and daintier than *C. latifolia*, reaching 3 ft. (1 m), and flowers earlier in the year, producing broader flatter bells in loose spikes, varying in colour from white to lavender-blue. It is a pretty plant for dry shade but can self-seed prolifically.

Two other species not normally recommended for shade but which seemed to thrive at the Garden House, are *Campanula lactiflora* (zone 5) and *C. poscharskyana* (zone 4). *Campanula lactiflora* is capable of reaching 5 ft. (1.5 m) in height and width with an equally large propensity for self-seeding as *C. persicifolia*. It is native to the alpine meadows of eastern Europe but will grow quite happily in some shade. Flowering mainly in midsummer in shades of white, pink or lavender-blue, it is the most spectacular of the species mentioned here but this vigorous growth does give it the propensity to flop over, especially in more shaded spots. To encourage branching and avoid the need for staking, shorten the length of stems in late spring and early summer. This will also prolong the flowering period as the lower the plant is cut back the later it will flower. In a large-scale natural garden this campanula would be a good choice. By contrast, the rampantly spreading trailing bellflower (*C. poscharskyana*) colonized the stonework of the walled garden at the Garden House in both shade and sun. Wherever it grew it flowered well, turning these vertical spaces a wonderful shade of lilac-blue in early summer.

Cardamine
lady's smock, cuckoo flower
Native to Europe
Zones vary by species
Growth habit Group 5, Low, spreading

Much as I love our native lady's smock, *Cardamine pratensis* (zone 3), it is best left for damp meadows or extensive naturalistic plantings. All the rest of the cardamines mentioned here come from central and southern Europe. This includes *C. raphanifolia* (zone 5), from southern Europe, which is a bigger version with darker lilac flowers than *C. pratensis* but lacks its grace. I once grew them together at the top of a little stream valley and they hybridized. The hybrid I called *C.* 'Wildside' and it had the colour and grace of *C. pratensis* but the size of *C. raphanifolia*, with enough hybrid vigour to outcompete both. It seeded true and spread all the way down the stream banks at the Garden House, intermingling with occasional clumps of *C. raphanifolia*

Cardamine pentaphyllos

Cassiope mertensiana and *Veronica cusickii*

snowdrops, producing a 6-in.-high (15 cm) mass of beautiful and dainty lilac-pink flowers. Therein lies the problem because flowering is inconsistent for no reason that I can ascertain. Some people have blamed pheasants for eating the buds but I have seen no evidence for that. Maybe I will try and feed it a bit more as I love the patches of cool colour this plant can bring to the garden.

Flowering in the main spring season comes *Cardamine pentaphyllos* (zone 6, formerly *Dentaria digitata*) with deeper pink flowers and a taller growth habit, reaching about 8 in. (20 cm). The leaves are more coarsely toothed than *C. quinquefolia*, but it forms a reliable, gently spreading clump with obvious affinities to lady's smock. *Cardamine heptaphylla* (zone 6, formerly *Dentaria pinnata*) is similar in size and habit but has pure white flowers in the form I have grown. *Cardamine kitaibelii* is also a similar size, but has nodding sprays of pale yellow flowers. These cardamines are all clump-formers of quiet charm but having grown these and many more over the years under different names, their current nomenclature leaves my head spinning.

to give a haze of various shades of lilac which proved to be a fabulous contrast to the long-flowering yellow candelabra primrose, *Primula helodoxa*, which shared this space.

Of the low-growing white-flowered cardamines I like *Cardamine waldsteinii* (zone 3) best, which grows only about 4 in. (10 cm) high with sprays of large flowers held just above the fresh green leaves. The size and number of flowers make quite a patch of white in the spring and it is a good companion for the blue single-flowered primrose 'Blue Sapphire'. An even better combination might be the dark blue single-flowered primrose 'Ingram's Blue', which has purple-flushed leaves.

Cardamine quinquefolia (zone 5) poses something of a problem. Growing slightly taller than *C. waldsteinii* it flowers in early spring along with *Cyclamen coum* and late

Cassiope

Native to arctic and north
 temperate montane regions
Zone 3
Growth habit Group 3,
 Tightly clumping evergreen

Cassiopes are very small heath-like evergreen shrubs, 6–12 in. (15–30 cm) high, in the rhododendron family. They have scale-like dark green leaves and in spring they produce an abundance of relatively large white, bell-shaped flowers. These plants will flower better in good light conditions but should not dry out in summer, so ideally should be planted in a partly shady spot. Some growers regularly cut back the top shoots to encourage basal growth. There are species from the Himalayas which are more upright in growth, while those from sub-polar regions tend to be prostrate. There are also numerous hybrids between them—all are worth trying. Naturally growing on moisture-retentive soils, stream banks or poolside would be a good home for them where, planted above the waterline, their roots could reach down to find the moisture. They will not appreciate being overgrown by taller neighbours though.

Chrysosplenium
Native to northern Europe and China
Zone 6
Growth habit Group 4, Prostrate

Completely prostrate spreading plants for shade are always welcome as they allow other slightly taller plants of graceful form to be appreciated to best advantage. The smallest chrysoplenium I know is the European golden saxifrage, *Chrysosplenium oppositifolium*, which carpets damp, shady places and stream banks with its tiny leaves. The small heads of yellow and green flowers resemble euphorbias and are produced in such numbers that they turn the ground yellow at flowering time in late spring and early summer. At the Garden House, it covered the lower sections of a north-facing 10-ft.-high (3 m) stone retaining wall and crept out into the bed beneath. I was happy to let it do so, but unless you are prepared to accept this plant's roving nature, it's probably best left to wilder areas of the shaded woodland.

The evergreen Chinese species, *Chrysosplenium davidianum* (zone 6), grows in exactly the same conditions but is larger all over. The leaves are darker green than our native species, which helps to make a correspondingly larger impact when in flower. It is capable of covering a lot of ground in ideal conditions, but is easily pulled out.

With dark evergreen foliage flushed reddish brown, *Chrysosplenium macrophyllum*

(zone 6) is also from China, but it is bigger and has leaves as large as those of bergenia. The flowers are held in the same flat heads as the other two species but are white with pink stamens on red stems. This plant has always seemed a bit untidy to me, and you need a lot of space to grow it, but I have seen it looking good (actually mistaking it for a bergenia) in Jimi Blake's wonderful woodland at Huntingbrook Gardens in Ireland, where he was growing it with *C. davidianum* on a large scale near the brook from which the garden takes its name.

Chrysosplenium davidianum

Clintonia

Native to North America
Zone 4
Growth habit Group 3, Tightly
 clumping evergreen

I grow two species of these low-growing evergreens, which need a cool, woodsy soil or a peat bed in partial shade. They have broad, strap-shaped leaves above which umbels of flowers appear in spring. From western North America, *Clintonia andrewsiana*, the red clintonia, is the most showy and the tallest of the two, reaching 12–18 in. (30–45 cm) in flower. It is striking both for its bright pink flowers and the dark blue fruits that follow. The more demure white clintonia (*C. umbellata*) from eastern North America makes almost prostrate mounds of foliage with umbels of white flowers 6 in. (15 cm) in height. It has its merits though, especially if grown among the less vigorous prostrate carpeting plants like those in Group 4.

Clintonia andrewsiana

Cornus unalaschkensis

Convallaria majalis

lily-of-the-valley
Native to temperate regions of
the northern hemisphere
Zone 3
Growth habit Group 4, Prostrate,
and Group 5, Low, spreading

In the nursery I have grown lilies-of-the-valley all my working life but I've rarely planted them in the garden. Desperately seeking some justification for this omission I can only come up with a wariness of the plant's reputation for spreading in most conditions but in the wilder parts of the woodland garden this is no excuse at all. I will remedy this omission but the only one I will plant near to anything remotely special will be 'Vic Pawlowski's Gold', named after a friend who was a magician of a propagator. This has the most strongly gold variegated leaves of any lily-of-the-valley I have seen.

Cornus canadensis

creeping dogwood
Native to northern Asia and
North America
Zone 2
Growth habit Group 4, Prostrate,
and Group 5, Low, spreading

Growing only 6 in. (15 cm) high and spreading by underground shoots, this herbaceous perennial could hardly be more different than the familiar flowering dogwood shrubs and trees. However, when it blooms in late spring and early summer, the similarity of the flower structure (really bracts) becomes apparent. The plants form a carpet of white amid fresh green leaves and the flowers are followed by bunches of bright red berries. In some years it is completely deciduous and the leaves can show good red autumn colour before dropping. But be warned: creeping dogwood is a vigorous

spreader in partial shade in the leafy acid soils that it likes, but any plants of Group 1 habit (upright, then arching) will happily grow through and clear of its carpet. *Cornus unalaschkensis* from the western side of North America is very similar.

Corydalis

fumewort
Native to the temperate
northern hemisphere
Zones vary by species
Growth habit Group 1, Upright, then arching; Group 5 Low, spreading (C. *flexuosa*)

An important genus for the woodland garden, *Corydalis* provides a reliable source of true blue flowers, mainly from the perennial species rather than the bulbous ones. Thirty years ago, this elusive colour was only occasionally encountered in corydalis, usually in the form of the difficult-to-grow and rarely seen *C. cashmeriana* (zone 5). But almost overnight (or so it seemed) *C. flexuosa* (zone 5) and *C. omeiana* (zone 6, introduced as *C. elata*) were released, proved easy to propagate, and reliable blue-flowered corydalis seemed to be everywhere.

Originally, three forms of *Corydalis flexuosa* were introduced, varying in the clarity of blue in their flowers and the amount of purple-red staining of their foliage. All were easy to grow forming spreading clumps, flowering in the spring at about 6 in. (15 cm) high, then dying down to below ground for the summer before reappearing with fresh leaves in the autumn. A slightly earlier introduction, but later to the United Kingdom, attributed to this species, 'Blue Panda', is a brighter blue but does not clump like those original forms, spreading gently around by self-seeding. *Corydalis omeiana* grew taller, up to 1 ft. (30 cm), flowering later in the summer for many weeks with scented clear blue flowers. 'Balang Mist' was the last *C. flexuosa* cultivar to be

Corydalis 'Blue Heron'

for much longer than either of its parents. Vigorous and easy, it grows to 1 ft. (30 cm) high, and we have even grown it in a grassy flower meadow. Other hybrids appeared about the same time in other gardens and all are similar, such as 'Craigton Blue', 'Tory Blue' and 'Spinners'. *Corydalis* 'Kingfisher' is a hybrid of *C. cashmeriana* (zone 6) and therefore does not have the vigour of other hybrids, slowly clumping up in my experience, but with larger flowers of electric blue over a long period. *Corydalis* 'Blue Heron' and 'Mount Rainier' were two seedlings collected in China by Dan Hinkley. 'Blue Heron' makes a slowly spreading clump of glaucous foliage that stays through the summer months, along with clear azure-blue flowers on red-flushed stems. It is not as easy to grow as the *C. flexuosa* cultivars but is worth finding a special place for it. 'Mount Rainier' has the most dazzlingly blue flowers of any corydalis I have grown but it seems to have a death wish in my garden and has slowly dwindled away.

There are still exciting blue corydalis trickling their way into cultivation, although many of them are treasures that require special care in the garden. Gothenburg Botanical Garden, surely the spiritual home of corydalis cultivation, has many of this new generation. *Corydalis pseudobarbisepala* has distinctive large leaflets and large rich blue flowers and also grows well in Peter Korn's sand beds. *Corydalis shensiana* has smaller paler blue flowers of a similar colour and style to *C. kokiana* which has a tenuous footing in UK gardens. A true star is *C. mucronipetala*, which was even seeding in the peat beds in Gothenburg. Ian and Maggi Young in Scotland, expert growers of all things bulbous, are having success with this species and my early efforts also appear promising. All grow well outside in Gothenburg, so are likely to be hardy to zone 6 or lower.

Away from the blues there are some lovely yellow corydalis, generally easy to grow, some almost too easy and others behaving as biennials or short-lived

introduced and has very pale blue flowers which form a lovely combination with its chocolate-brown young growth.

It wasn't long before gardeners and growers were finding hybrids (all zones 6 to 7), between these three species, as well as with newer species coming from China. *Corydalis* 'Wildside Blue' (*C. flexuosa* × *C. elata*) originated in our garden and produces its dark blue, highly scented flowers

Corydalis malkensis

Corydalis scouleri

perennials. Falling into the former category due to its prolific self-seeding is *Corydalis lutea* (zone 6, syn. *Pseudofumaria lutea*), but it has the qualities of fresh green feathery foliage and a nearly continuous display of bright yellow flowers from summer until the frosts of late autumn. I have seen great-looking stone walls completely studded with this plant, but have so far lacked the courage to introduce it to my own garden. *Corydalis ochroleuca* (syn. *Pseudofumaria alba*) is hardy to zone 5 and equally long flowering and, to my eye, more refined. I love its sprays of beautifully scented, yellow-tipped white flowers. It also self-seeds but not as prolifically as *C. lutea*, and it forms upright clumps about 1 ft. (30 cm) high. Another corydalis that relies on self-seeding to spread—although I could never have too much of it—is *C. cheilanthifolia* (zone 6). This forms evergreen rosettes of dark green leaves as finely divided as any fern (often purple flushed through the winter) from which the central spikes of clear yellow flowers rise in spring to 6–9 in. (15–22 cm). It likes a cool spot

Trilliums and corydalis

Corydalis mucronipetala

Corydalis 'Mount Rainier'

in half shade. The taller *C. nobilis* (zone 4) grows 1 ft. (30 cm) high, with yellow flowers tipped purple-brown. It is an excellent garden plant in the more continental climate of Scandinavia, but is unfortunately rarely seen in the United Kingdom. It is a beautiful plant when happy.

The tuberous and bulbous corydalis are a large group. *Corydalis solida* (zone 6) is perhaps the most frequently encountered and comes in a range of colours that can rival the impact of any collection of spring bulbs. I am told the secret to growing this species successfully is to replant the bulbs every year into fresh potting soil just as the old leaves are dying down for the summer. Aquatic plant baskets are ideal for the purpose. Bigger and coarser in all its parts from *C. solida*, *C. bulbosa* (zone 5) has scented flowers and for a semi-shady spot under tall shrubs can be very pretty especially in its white form. The best stands of both of these species I have seen were growing with relatively little competition from other plants so I wonder if this explains my lack of success as I tend to prefer plants that mingle. In any case both have died down entirely by early summer.

Many of the other tuberous corydalis are toys to be cherished in a special spot but the very beautiful *Corydalis malkensis* (zone 7) can be an exception. It has large white flowers and can carpet the ground in a lightly shaded spot and will even seed itself gently around. Two other fleshy-rooted corydalis which self-seed to the point that some plantspeople will not grow them are *C. linstowiana* (zone 7) and *C. shimienensis* (zone 5). *Corydalis linstowiana* has a small carrot-like root and blue-grey dissected foliage that is present all summer but not too dense that other bulbous plants cannot push through it. The racemes of highly scented, pale blue flowers are compact at first, then elongate with age. It flowers for much of the summer as does *C. shimienensis*, which has more copious ferny foliage and sprays of purple-red flowers, a colour repeated on the stems and the flecking on the leaves. It behaves as an annual or biennial and is sometimes sold as *C.* 'Blackberry Wine'.

The largest species is *Corydalis scouleri* (zone 6) from the Pacific Northwest. Its very lacy, fresh green foliage can reach nearly 5 ft. (1.5 m) high in a moist soil in full or partial shade, and it can form sizeable colonies where happy. The small (relative to the size of the plant) pink flowers are borne in racemes held well above the foliage in early summer.

Dicentra
bleeding heart
Native to eastern Asia and North America
Zone 5
Growth habit Group 5, Low, spreading

All the dicentras have lovely foliage and the ones I tend to grow are easy, reliable perennials for the woodland garden. The common name refers to their pendent, roughly heart-shaped flowers but the original gardener's bleeding heart, *Dicentra spectabilis*, has now been reclassified as *Lamprocapnos spectabilis*. Those that remain as *Dicentra* are lower-growing perennials with an additional two spring ephemeral species which retire below ground soon after flowering.

The most commonly encountered dicentras in gardens are cultivars or hybrids of *Dicentra eximea* and *D. formosana*. Both of these species have creeping rhizomes and can cover considerable space so are best suited to larger plantings, but their hybrid offspring are more amenable to confinement. All have feathery foliage that is often grey-blue and they make gently spreading clumps 8–12 in. (20–30 cm) high with locket-like flowers in white, pink or red which hang from flowering stems held just above the foliage. There are

Dicentra cucullaria

many named forms; among them 'Langtrees' has very blue foliage and white flowers; 'Bacchanal' is taller with deep red flowers; 'Stuart Boothman' has silvery grey, very finely divided foliage and pink flowers. Care should be taken with this last cultivar to make sure it doesn't self-seed as the seedlings can have much coarser foliage which will soon overrun its classy parent.

One of the gems of the Alpine Garden Society's show benches is *Dicentra peregrina* which comes outside the scope of this book requiring as it does very specialized conditions, but this has been used as a parent to create some very refined hybrids which are much easier to grow. *Dicentra* 'King of Hearts' has very finely divided leaves, a compact habit and large pink-red flowers; 'Gothenburg' is similar with clean light pink flowers and seeds true to type, while the newer 'Burning Hearts' has lacier foliage and almost red flowers. The white 'Ivory Hearts' will also self-seed but

appears to be a little more tricky to grow well. All of them are worth a place among the treasures of the woodland bed. In the same series, bred by Gothenburg Botanical Garden and released in 2014 is, 'Love Hearts' has white flowers tipped in pink.

Two dicentras from North American woods, for whom the term "spring ephemerals" could have been invented, are *Dicentra canadensis* and *D. cucullaria*. Both are superficially similar, emerging in early spring with compact clumps of glaucous dissected foliage, quickly followed by sprays of white flowers on 6–8 in. (15–20 cm) stems, before equally quickly dying down and retreating below ground to their sweetcorn-like swollen roots for the rest of the year. The main difference is the shape of the flower; in *D. cucullaria* they form the shape of a V and in *D. canadensis* they are heart shaped (and sweetly scented). Despite their ephemerality I wouldn't be without them.

Dicentra 'King of Hearts'

Diphyllea cymosa

umbrella leaf
Zone 7
Native to eastern North America
Growth habit Group 6, Bold foliage plants

A handsome foliage plant from the mountainous woods of the southeastern states of North America, umbrella leaf needs a cool site and will grow up to 4 ft. (1.2 m) high in good conditions. In early summer, surprisingly large white flowers appear in dense rounded clusters, followed by blue berries on red stalks. The foliage can also show good autumn colour. Plant it with ferns, hostas, rodgersias and smilacinas, where it will happily mingle.

Diphyllea cymosa and sensitive fern (*Onoclea sensibilis*)

Disporum

fairy bells
Zones vary by species
Native to Asia
Growth habit Group 1, Upright, then arching

I have not had the chance to grow some of the newly introduced disporums, but those ones I do grow, I value a lot. Crug Farm Plants has introduced several species; the ones I know vary in size from 1–6 ft. (30 cm–2 m) in height. Two of the smaller ones

Disporum longistylum 'Green Giant'

Dodecatheon meadia 'Alba'

are variegated, one very easy to please, the other quite difficult.

The easy variegated species is *Disporum sessile* 'Variegatum' (zone 4), which grows to 1 ft. (30 cm) high and has white-and-grey longitudinally striped leaves and in spring produces narrow cream bells that hang in pairs from the leaf axils of the branching stems. Grow this plant for the foliage, because the flowers are overwhelmed by the striking variegation of the leaves, and don't put it too close to smaller plants as it will spread from quite vigorous rhizomes. I find the scarcer 'Rick's Form' much more difficult to please. The gold variegation is very striking but it is not a vigorous garden plant. One to best cherish on the alpine show benches perhaps.

I bought *Disporum uniflorum* (zone 4) when it was still called *D. flavens*, a name which more accurately describes the colour of the flower. The bright yellow flowers in early summer are quite large and hang noticeably from the ends of the 2-ft. (60-cm) upright stems, which arch gracefully at the tips. The bright green leaves clasp the stems and create pillars of very fine foliage. This is a good choice to provide contrast with epimediums and trilliums.

Of similar habit but considerably bigger than *Disporum uniflorum* is *D. longistylum* 'Green Giant' (zone 7). It takes time to build up to full size but when full grown it has the air of a bamboo crossed with a solomon's seal, with greenish yellow flowers smothering the top of the clump. Slightly smaller is *D. cantoniense* 'Night Heron' (zone 7), with purple new foliage and stems that form a sumptuous contrast with those same yellow-green flowers. In both cases the thickest stems emerge in early spring and so are susceptible to late frosts. Established clumps will soon shoot again even if repeatedly caught by cold nights but the shoots become progressively thinner and weaker. To ensure plants are able to reach their full height, provide these plants with a sheltered site or protection of some sort.

Dodecatheon

shooting star
Zones vary by species
Native mainly to North America
Growth habit Group 3, Tightly clumping

Most dodecatheons prefer a cool moist soil, especially in spring, in sun or part-shade. Those suitable for woodland conditions usually have primula-like leaves and upright stems carrying heads of swept-back flowers that resemble pink or white cyclamen. All the dodecatheon have similar flower shapes and all die back below ground by midsummer, so planting many together can leave bare patches later in the season. This can be resolved by growing them among autumn-flowering gentians or other plants, such as begonias, which emerge very late in the season.

Dodecatheon meadia (zone 3) is an easy species to grow reaching 18–24 in. (45–60 cm) in height with rose-coloured flowers, lighter at their tips. There is a white-flowered form, *D. meadia* forma *album*. In this species the basal leaves stand upright but in some other species the leaves lie flat on the ground.

The Californian native *Dodecatheon clevelandii* ssp. *insulare* (zone 7) has these low-growing leaves and is a much dwarfer plant, but the foliage habit gives it a much neater appearance. *Dodecatheon hendersonii* (zone 7) also has foliage that lies close to horizontal. Both of these species need moisture in the spring but well-drained conditions in the summer, not easy to replicate in all gardens.

Dodecatheon dentatum (zone 5) is one of the babies of the genus, with its leaves barely reaching 3 in. (7 cm) high. It spreads by underground stolons and is native to moist woodlands, in shady places along streams and wet meadows. Its small size and the fact that it dies back early in the season means it can easily be grown with other small plants despite its running habit. The flower stems can reach 12–17 in. (30–42 cm) high, although they may be smaller than this, and they bear nodding white flowers in spring.

Epimedium

bishop's hat
Zone 5, except as noted
Native mainly to China
Growth habit Group 2, Low, clumping, except as noted

This is an important genus of low-growing, mostly evergreen perennials that flower in midspring. When I first started gardening over forty years ago there were perhaps only twenty epimediums in our gardens. Thanks largely to the work of nurserymen like Darrell Probst in Massachusetts and Robin and Sue White from the sadly missed Blackthorn Nursery in the United Kingdom (with considerable help from Mikinori Ogisu from Japan who collected many new species in the wild) there are now over 200 listed in the current RHS Plantfinder, with many more hybrids being

Epimedium 'Wildside Ruby'

Epimedium 'Arctic Wings'

Epimedium fargesii

introduced each year. They are prolific at self-hybridizing so if you grow several together and the seed has somewhere to germinate, new crosses are likely to emerge. Species and named clones need to be divided (best done in late summer) if you want to keep them true to name.

The "old guard" of epimediums are almost indestructible woodland plants forming 1-ft.-high (30 cm), slowly spreading dense clumps of pinnate leaves which are often attractively bronze on first emerging and topped by sprays of nodding spurred flowers in spring. They are easy, reliable and a good weed suppressant as well as being very handsome and can even grow in grass under trees (although this isn't recommended). Were I to restrict myself to just one of each of the colours available from these older varieties I would choose *E.* ×*youngianum* 'Niveum' (white flowers), *E.* ×*versicolor* 'Sulphureum' (yellow flowers), *E.* ×*versicolor* 'Versicolor' (orange-red flowers) and the evergreen *E. perralchium* 'Wisley' (bright yellow

flowers). The first three all have the characteristic bronzed young growth. I also like all the *E. grandiflorum* cultivars which grow very well in our wetter climate but are not as successful in drier conditions.

The newer species introduced from China and elsewhere in Asia have considerably raised the bar for both colour and form. Some have much larger flowers, many have exquisitely mottled and marbled leaves, others bring completely new flower colours to the table, while some are much taller with masses of flowers on the long flowering stems. With their willingness to hybridize its not surprising that an ever-increasing number of hybrid cultivars are emerging.

There is always a catch though. First, not all of the new species are as easy as the older epimediums—some need just the right placement in part shade in a cool spot which isn't sodden. I grow mine on part-shady banks (which provide drainage) in moisture-retentive soil (which provides a cool root-run). Second, some of the species—like *Epimedium brachyrrhizum* and *E. ogisui*—flower early in the season and so are vulnerable to late frosts. Growing any of them under cover will produce the best results when their individually beautiful flowers can develop and be appreciated without being compromised by the weather, but is obviously not an option for everyone. Growing them in containers also leaves the plants more open to attack from vine weevils (unless chemical or biological controls are taken), which adore epimediums as much as I do. Planted in the ground, natural predation controls weevil numbers to some extent.

Epimedium davidii was one of the first of these Chinese species to be introduced. It makes an evergreen clump 8–12 in. (20–30 cm) high, topped by many bright yellow flowers. Some forms have purplish copper young foliage which adds considerably to the flowering effect. There is also a dwarf form which is useful among other small treasures in a raised bed. There is little to choose from between the pale yellow *E.*

Epimedium fargesii 'Pink Constellation'

lischichenii and *E. franchetti* 'Brimstone Butterfly', as both have bronzed spring foliage to enhance the flowers. Among the other yellows *E. ecalcaratum* is especially good, like a very fine *E. davidii* with more open graceful, bright-yellow flower sprays.

Epimedium acuminatum has beautiful mottled leaves and wide arching sprays of large two-tone flowers, the widely splayed sepals paler in colour than the inner petals. In this species it has usually lavender-lilac sepals and purple petals, but has also produced a pure white flowered form named 'Galaxy'. Another sister seedling

Epimedium hybrids

As with erythroniums, the epimedium hybrids are often better garden plants than their species parents. This is a selection of those I think are the most distinct.

White

'Amanogawa' makes clumps 12–18 in. (30–45 cm) high, reliably topped by long-lasting sprays of broad-sepalled white flowers with brown petals.

'Milky Way' grows to 1 ft. (30 cm), with masses of backswept, starry white flowers set off among bronzed chocolate young foliage.

'Arctic Wings' is a free-flowering hybrid of *Epimedium latisepalum* and *E. ogisui* and with two such parents is hardly surprising that it presents beautifully formed large white flowers—with a little hybrid vigour thrown in for good measure.

Yellow

'Flowers of Sulphur' grows 8–12 in. (20–30cm) high topped in spring with masses of large pale lemon-yellow flowers.

'Golden Eagle' is taller, to 2 ft. (60 cm), with bronze young foliage over which the tall arching sprays of wide spidery bright yellow flowers appear.

Orange

'Amber Queen' was a real colour break, bred by Blackthorn Nursery, with masses of soft orange flowers for many weeks on 18-in. (45-cm) stems. In an overly sunny position the flowers do bleach a bit; if this occurs, move the plant to a shadier spot.

'Wildside Amber' appeared spontaneously at our nursery and was clearly a seedling of 'Amber Queen'. It grows taller with larger flowers, flushed more distinctly red on the petals, and has the added advantage of bronzed mottled young foliage.

Pink and Purple

'Enchantress' has been around the longest of these hybrids. It is a hybrid of *Epimedium leptorrhizum* and has inherited that species' attributes of abundant flowers and handsome spring foliage. Growing 8–12 in. (20–30 cm) high, it has broad pink sepals and purple petals.

'Kaguyahime' is a wonderful foliage plant when its leaves are purple-bronze flushed in the spring at the same time as the airy sprays of lavender flowers. Growing 18–24 in. (45–60 cm) high, it is taller than many other epimediums and so needs a bit of space.

Blends

'Buff Beauty' is another Wildside seedling and a distinct colour break, with large broad-sepalled flowers of an even buff-ochre colour set off among chocolate-brown young leaves. It has a compact habit to 8–12 in. (20–30cm).

'Firedragon' has large orange and red flowers.

'Madame Butterfly' has pale yellow sepals with red-pink inner petals.

'Wildside Ruby' is a selection I made for its outstanding purple young foliage, more intense than any other epimedium I have grown. The flowers, though numerous, are small, rose-pink and yellow.

Epimedium leptorrhizum
'Mariko'

Epimedium 'Amber
Queen'

Epimedium grandiflorum
'Wildside Red'

Epimedium
'Buckland Spider'

sure all of these are going to play a part in future breeding programmes, as might *E. macrosepalum*. This uncommon species has a running growth habit, and it boasts the broadest sepals of any epimedium I have seen, a strong rose-pink in colour. It isn't very free flowering but it does not take much imagination to see it has importance as a parent for future hybrids.

A few more Chinese species are very beautiful but may be of marginal usefulness because of their early flowering unless you have a sheltered site where the morning sun will not damage them after a frost. *Epimedium ogisui* (zone 6) has a gently creeping habit and grows to 6–8 in. (15–20 cm) high with sprays of large white flowers and copper mottled and marbled young leaves. *Epimedium leptorrhizum* 'Mariko' is very similar except for rose-pink sepals and white petals. *Epimedium brachyrrhizum* grows a bit taller and is more clump forming. It has broader leaves that emerge the colour of chocolate milk among which the soft rose-pink flowers are set. Lastly, *E. latisepalum* highlights both the joys and challenges of some of these newer species. Grown with protection under cover the large white flowers of beautiful proportions and form are an absolute delight, but in less than ideal conditions outside it can be quite a disappointment, looking rather weather-beaten.

with typical coloured flowers is 'Persian Carpet'. It has particularly well-marked leaves which remain colourful throughout the winter.

Among the new colours brought onto the market is *Epimedium ×omeinse* which is a naturally occurring hybrid and the two cultivars of it I grow have significantly different flower colour. 'Akame' has large red flowers tipped with yellow on the inner petals. 'Stormcloud' is rather gloomy, an acquired taste with chocolate-brown and purple flowers. *Epimedium wushanense* is one of the taller species, capable of reaching 3 ft. (1 m) in height and producing hundreds of pale yellow flowers on its branching stems. The variety 'Caramel' is a colour break of the species, less vigorous, with wide ochre flowers tipped bronze-red on the petals, set off against chocolate-bronze foliage in the spring. I'm

Galax aphylla

wandflower, beetleweed, galaxy
Native to the Appalachian Mountains
Zone 5
Growth habit Group 3, Tightly
    clumping evergreen

A rarely seen evergreen in our gardens, wandflower forms patches of rounded glossy leaves that turn crimson in the winter. It grows to 6 in. (15 cm) high topped by the narrow spikes of white flowers that give the plant its most familiar common

Galax aphylla

name. This plant used to thrive in a nursery I worked in when I first left school and has stayed in my memory ever since. It must be propagated by division, but in my experience it is not easy to do so. Grow on acid woodland soils.

Gentiana

gentian
Zone 6
Native to temperate regions
Growth habit Group 3, Tightly
    clumping mostly evergreen,
    to Group 7, Tall, clumping

The spring-flowering gentians are not suitable for the woodland garden because they need good light levels to flower well. Even the low-growing autumn gentians are best where they they can receive good light for part of the day and also need an acid soil. I grow some of these in dappled shade and on north-facing banks away from the drip lines of trees and they have done very well—but I can't pretend to have an expert's knowledge. 'Blue Silk' has

Gentiana asclepiadea

flowered reliably, covering itself with dark blue trumpets in midautumn. It only grows to 2 in. (5 cm) and would not appreciate being overgrown by taller plants as early autumn approaches, but is best in the company of spring-flowering bulbs and perennials which have died down by late summer.

Gentiana asclepiadea, the willow gentian, is a much more amenable species. Native to eastern and central Europe, it puts out willowy growth of dark green leaves 2–3 ft. (60–80 cm) high with the typical gentian trumpets springing from the axils of the leaves in the upper sections in late summer. They are normally midblue but can be white or pink in named clones. Its arching, even sprawling, growth habit makes it difficult to combine with other smaller plants unless they have already died down or are tolerant of being overgrown (such as spring-flowering shade-tolerant perennials like primroses). Another option is to grow the willow gentian among taller neighbours or under widely spaced shrubs where it would create a very natural-looking planting.

Geranium

cranesbill
Native to temperate regions worldwide
Zones vary by species
Growth habit Group 5, Low, spreading

Most cranesbills are really sun lovers, but there are quite a few species which are at home in the semi-shade of the woodland garden. If you want a low-maintenance garden with perennials and the site is only partially shaded, this genus is where you should look first. Among its ranks are some very easy groundcover plants capable of smothering weeds. They are however not very selective and will equally smother less vigorous plants.

Those well suited to this purpose in light shade (also worth trying in dry shade) are

Geranium endressii (various shades of pink, zone 4), *G. himalayense* (deep blue, zone 4), *G. ibericum* (purple-blue, zone 5), *G. macrorrhizum* (pink or white, zone 4), *G.* ×*oxonianum* (shades of pink, zone 5), *G.* ×*cantabrigiense* (lower-growing pink or white, zone 5). *Geranium clarkei* (zone 4), sold under the cultivar names of 'Kashmir' followed by either 'Blue', 'Pink', 'Purple' or 'White', are all more refined and worthy of a place in any garden.

Hardy to zone 5 and both to be planted with extreme caution are *Geranium nodosum*, which not only runs but self-seeds prolifically, and *G. procurrens*, which roots from every node of its long trailing stems in the same way as creeping buttercup (*Ranunculus repens*). Back in the heyday of *Geranium* sales we used to sell masses of this latter plant on the strength of our reasonable and accurate description of it

Geranium sylvaticum

Tulipa sprengeri and *Geranium asphodeloides*

as a 'rampageous beauty', but have often wondered how many of our customers regretted introducing it into their gardens. This species did pass on its lovely flowers to two exceptional hybrids that have more polite garden manners in the form of 'Ann Folkard' and 'Salome'. Many other hybrids like 'Blue Cloud', 'Brookside', 'Dilys', 'Johnson's Blue', 'Joy' and others would certainly be worth trying in semi-shade. *Geranium asphodeloides* (zone 6) is also worth considering if you want a wilder look, due to its habit of weaving through neighbouring plants. Self-seeding and with plentiful small flowers, it is a species that benefits from being cut back in midsummer, so it is an ideal candidate for growing in thin grass.

There are some *Geranium* species for whom the woodland is their natural home. The first is *G. sylvaticum* (zone 4), a clump-forming species growing to about 30 in. (75 cm). It flowers in the spring and I recommend its cultivars 'Amy Doncaster' (a good dark blue), 'Album' (pristine white) and 'Baker's Pink' (a good pale pink). Another spring-flowering cranesbill of

class is the North American *G. maculatum* (zone 4), which is of similar height but somehow more graceful with elegantly deployed lilac-pink flowers. There is a very good white form, 'Album', and one with good purple-brown leaves and pink flowers, 'Espresso', which as with many foliage plants of this colour, is more pronounced in less shady spots.

My last *Geranium* is one I look forward to as much as any other. It is *G. libani* × *G. peloponnesiacum* (zone 6). A plant listed under this cross has recently been given the name *G.* 'Solitaire'. Unlike any of the others mentioned it is semi-tuberous, quickly dying back below ground after flowering in midspring—but what a flowering! At 12–18 in. (30–45 cm) high in flower, with masses of large clear lilac-blue flowers with darker veins this has few equals. The colour positively glows in dappled sunlight and it does seem to appreciate a slightly cooler site. Large patches of it were a great success in an open position in the old north-facing bulb meadow at the Garden House where it received no direct sunlight when in growth.

Glaucidium palmatum
Japanese wood poppy
Native to Japan
Zone 5
Growth habit Group 6, Bold foliage plants

One of the gems of the woodland garden and—as with so many Japanese plants—imbued with that undeniable quality of "class". Intolerant of high summer temperatures, the best Japanese wood poppies I have ever seen have been in the cooler climate of Scotland where they formed clumps nearly 3 ft. (1 m) high and wide. Needs cool shade and a moisture-retentive woodsy soil. There is an almost more beautiful pure white variety, 'Album'.

Glaucidium palmatum 'Album'

Haberlea rhodopensis
Native to eastern Europe
Zone 5
Growth habit Group 3, Tightly clumping evergreen

If you have an earth-filled dry stone wall or a north-facing bank backed by soil, then haberleas would be an excellent choice for planting there. Very similar in habit and size to ramondas, this plant has rosettes of dark green glossy leaves which form a tight clump. In dry spells these leaves can look very sad, all curled and crisped, but usually a spell of wet weather miraculously recovers them. Branching sprays of dark blue slightly tubular flowers with white throats held just above the leaves reward successful growers.

Haberlea rhodopensis

Hacquetia epipactis

Native to Europe
Zone 5
Growth habit Group 3, Tightly clumping

This is another low-growing clump former with fresh green scallop-shaped leaves. The spring "flowers" are composed of a central boss of insignificant fertile flowers surrounded by a ruff of yellow-green bracts. It may not sound very enticing but the overall effect is of a charming posey of lime-green. It will gently seed itself around if there is anywhere for the seeds to germinate but it has never been a problem in my garden. There is a variegated form which I have never felt the need to grow (but then I am not a great variegated fan).

Helleborus

hellebore
Native to Europe through to the Caucasus
Zones vary by species
Growth habit Group 2, Low, clumping

There cannot be a gardener anywhere who doesn't grow or at least know what a hellebore is, so I won't insult anybody's intelligence by describing the commonly seen Lenten rose, *Helleborus ×hybridus*. Forty years ago there were few colours available and those had to be propagated by division, and being slow to increase were therefore expensive to buy. Over the intervening decades colours have been refined and seed strains developed which breed true and so the prices have dropped

Hacquetia epipactis 'Thor'

Helleborus ×ericsmithii
'Silvermoon'

considerably. There are now good yellows, whites, pinks bordering on reds, smokey blues, purple-blacks, variously spotted, picotees, doubles and blends of all of these. It's always worth trying to buy a hellebore when it is in bloom because although flower forms have been immeasurably improved by careful selective breeding there are still many hellebores on the market which perpetuate the old fault of two of the five petals being slightly misshapen.

Helleborus orientalis and *H. ×hybridus* (both zone 4) will almost certainly self-seed in your garden though I would sound a note of caution. Exciting as it is for your plants to spread there is an argument for keeping individual hellebores reasonably well spaced, much like ferns and grasses, to allow the plants to flower more prolifically and where their domed graceful habit can be better appreciated. If you allow these plants to self-seed without any control the ensuing mass of seedlings results in each

individual having smaller flowers with less of them, and the summer foliage effect is a rather charmless, shapeless ground-covering carpet. Remove most of the seedlings, especially those close to the parent plant, to avoid this happening.

I have never had much success with the Christmas rose, *Helleborus niger* (zone 3), perhaps because I have always gardened on acid soils and it has a reputed preference for alkaline conditions, but its cross with *H. ×sternii* produced *H. ×ericsmithii* (zone 7) which seems to be more robust. In its best forms this cross can boast beautiful silver mottled and splashed leaves and many maroon-red flowering stems carrying many large saucer-shaped, creamy off-white flowers. In the variety 'Ruby Glow' the maroon-red of the flowering stems continues onto the reverse of the petals and this colouration is still strong long after the flowers are past their best. So long-lasting is this spring display that it can be hard to know when to cut back the flowering stems at the base, a necessary job after flowering which encourages healthy new growth to develop as quickly as possible. The positive characteristics of this plant were partly involved in a ten-year breeding programme carried out by Rodney Davey in Devon to produce the stunning 'Anna's Red' (zone 4). The marbled foliage, flushed pink when young, is followed by almost red outward-facing flowers of beautiful shape and substance on red stems, a winning combination if ever there was one. Pink-flowered 'Penny's Pink' (zone 4) came out of the same breeding and has the same characteristics. Both are now being sold worldwide.

The foliage of the hellebores already mentioned might be considered a bit heavy for some tastes or situations, in which case *Helleborus purpurascens* (zone 7) is an option. This has lighter green, more dissected leaves and flowers of a more subdued nature. In the form I grow these flowers are about 2 in. (5 cm) across, flushed purple on their reverse and blue-green on the inside. It is a plant of more quiet charm that combines very easily and sympathetically with virtually all other spring-flowering woodlanders.

For those gardeners who like a challenge *Helleborus thibetanus* (zone 7) might fit the bill. In the United Kingdom this is generally considered a slightly tricky plant to grow well in the garden because it demands some shade, drainage and dryness in the summer with shelter in the spring. Having seen an enormous clump growing in what seemed ordinary conditions in a Toronto garden I wonder whether it might be happier in a more continental climate. At its best this deciduous species is very beautiful in early spring when its pale pink-white flowers finely striped with pink are set off among fresh green-fingered young leaves that are bronzed when they first emerge. At this time it resembles a giant flowered cardamine more than a typical hellebore and so offers more opportunities for successfully blending with other woodlanders.

Heloniopsis
Native to Japan, Korea and Taiwan
Zone 6
Growth habit Group 3, Tightly
     clumping evergreen

Heloniopsis is valuable as a low-growing evergreen with glossy fresh green leaves growing about 6 in. (15 cm) high. In spring plants produce short racemes of small, narrow-petalled lily-like flowers on stems rising above the clumps. The protruding anthers give the flowers a rather spikey appearance. Both *H. breviscapa* and *H. orientalis* are very similar in foliage and both have pink or lilac-pink flowers, but the latter's flower spikes are curved. *Heloniopsis umbellata* has narrower foliage and is slightly shorter than the above species with ball-like heads of white flowers, at least in the form I grow. Shorter still is *H. kawanoi*, a dwarf species, the foliage barely reaching 2 in. (5 cm), so place it along with similar small treasures. The flowering stems reach about 4 in. (10 cm) with lilac-purple flowers.

Hepatica
Native to Europe, Asia and
     eastern North America
Zones vary by species
Growth habit Group 3, Tightly
     clumping, mostly evergreen

Hepaticas generally seem to prefer alkaline soils. On the acidic soils where I have gardened I have found them to be infuriatingly inconsistent. I have planted out three groups in what I thought were identical conditions and two slowly faded away while the third thrived. They are worth persevering with though as when they do thrive they can provide reliable patches of startling colour in the spring, with handsome foliage on compact clumps thrown in as well. Partial shade and a cool spot that is not wet are the recommended conditions.

Hepatica nobilis 'Pico's Strain'

The commonly available hepatica are seed-raised strains of *Hepatica nobilis* (zone 5), which is a lime lover and usually found in the alpine sections of many garden centres or catalogues in the spring. They can be white, shades of blue or shocking pink and are not expensive, so considering how many have been sold it is surprising they aren't more commonly seen in gardens—clearly I am not the only one who struggles to keep them going. *Hepatica nobilis* var. *japonica* is reputedly more tolerant of acid soils and in the strain I grow has notably more silvered leaves. Well-marked leaves and large flowers in various shades are the hallmark of *H. nobilis* 'Pico's Strain'. The many double forms, so beloved of growers in Asia, can be very expensive and are best appreciated in the alpine house.

Hepatica americana (zone 3) is less flamboyant than *H. nobilis* but has considerable charm and is hardier. Both in flower and foliage it has a frailer, less heavy appearance with many very pale lavender-blue flowers amid bronze-grey marbled leaves (hence its common name of liverleaf) in spring. *Hepatica transsilvanica* (zone 5) is larger in all its parts than the others mentioned so far. It spreads by underground rhizomes, making clumps about 8 in. high × 12 in. wide (20 × 30 cm). Generally it is an easier plant to please in the open garden with bigger flowers and more petals of usually a good lilac-blue colour. There are also pink- and white-flowered forms to search out as well

Hepatica ×*media* 'Sue White'

as the cultivar 'Elison Spence', which has a central boss of staminoid petals.

Of similar size to *Hepatica transsilvanica* are its hybrids with *H. nobilis, H. ×media* (zone 5). In its best forms these are some of the very best hepaticas for the garden, with large beautifully shaped flowers of an exquisite lavender-blue. The form 'Ballardii' sets the bar very high but is not easy to find. 'Harvington Beauty' comes close and there is also a very good dark blue double, 'Millstream Merlin', as well as the superlative soft pink 'Sue White'.

In recent years hybrids between *Hepatica maxima* and *H. nobilis* have been given the name *H. ×schlyteri* (zone 6) and these boast the biggest flowers in the genus. These plants make leafy clumps 8 in. (20 cm) high and 1 ft. (30 cm) wide, and are distinct in having glossy green foliage and very noticeable large green bracts below each flower. In the garden of their creator I have seen these hepaticas growing well and spectacular in flower: 'Blue Max' (dark blue), 'The Bride' (white) and 'Red Max'.

Heuchera
coral bells
Native to North America
Zone 4
Growth habit Group 2, Low, clumping

This group of semi-evergreen perennials are mainly grown for their foliage which, thanks to extensive breeding work over the last two decades, has produced a bewildering range of subtle mottlings and leaf colours. These range from pale lemon-yellows through grays to rich purples, reds and browns. Heucheras are not plants you can plant and forget about because they form increasingly woody basal stems which every few years need to be dug and replanted, a process best carried out in late summer or very early autumn. Their tall thin flowering stems supporting tiny fringed bell-like flowers also become

Mixed *Heuchera*

untidy when the flowers have faded unless regularly deadheaded. Much worse though, if your garden is prone to them, are the attacks of vine weevil larvae. These soil-dwelling grubs eat the roots of coral bells and can kill a large clump in a single season if undetected. If these limitations are not too onerous then there are few low, easy woodland plants that can provide such good foliage effects for such a long season as these new heucheras.

Hosta 'Gold Standard' with *Gymnocarpium dryopteris* 'Plumosum' in the foreground.

Hosta

plantain lily
Native to northern Asia
Zone 3
Growth habit Group 6, Bold foliage plants

Rather like the cliché where all buses arrive at the same time, the heucheras are followed here with another group of first-rate, easy foliage plants in the form of hostas. These plants—apart from being infamously attacked by slugs and snails—can be planted and left alone and then they improve year on year with virtually no attention. An unbelievable range of sizes and colours are now available from 8 in. (20 cm) to nearly 3 ft. (1 m) high and choosing which to grow is a matter of personal taste. I would say however that in a larger space, hostas are always going to look more natural and at home if the individual varieties, of whatever colour, are planted in groups as large as possible.

An established hosta clump is adept at smothering weeds, so it may come as a surprise to learn you can actually grow some early spring-flowering woodlanders among the hosta roots. You might also think that below the canopy of those large leaves the soil in summer would be parched, but thanks to the gutter-like leaf stalks and the form of the leaves, a significant amount of rainfall is channeled back to the centre of the plant. This coupled with the fact that the finer feeding roots are mainly situated around the periphery of the clump (where the majority of the rainfall is deposited) means there is usually enough soil amid the thicker central roots to provide a congenial home for early spring flowers like snowdrops and wood anemones. However, a little forethought and common sense is required to successfully pull off this double act. It works best with later-leafing hostas, like *Hosta sieboldiana* and accompanying plants that flower very early. Don't attempt to plant anything into an established hosta clump, instead either plant the two unlikely bedfellows close together when small, or plant a smaller spreading plant, like wood anemones, at the outside edge of the established hosta and hope with time it will colonize under the leaves as well as away from them. I have found that this principle works not only with hostas but also with rodgersias, veratrums, zantedeschias and to a lesser extent with rheums and smilacinas.

Impatiens

balsam
Native to China and Tibet
Zones vary by species
Growth habit Group 2, Low, clumping

Impatiens omeiana (zone 6) from China is a handsome foliage plant that grows about 18 in. (45 cm) high. It forms spreading clumps of upright stems set along their lengths with narrow dark green, gently scallop-edged leaves with distinctive yellow midribs and red leaf stalks. Starting in midsummer, orange-yellow helmeted flowers emerge from the upper leaf axils. It is easy to grow in a cool spot but it can

swamp more delicate neighbours. There are several forms in cultivation varying in the intensity of the green, yellow or red leaf colouration.

The Blue Diamond impatiens—also called sapphire jewelweed—is less reliably perennial even in a sheltered spot, but usually maintains its presence by self-seeding. It is native to Tibet's Namchabarwa Canyon, which is apparently twice as deep as the Grand Canyon, and consequently has the challenging but lyrical botanical name of *Impatiens namchabarwensis* (zone 9). In a cool, moist and shady site Blue Diamond impatiens will flower from spring to the first frosts of autumn, quickly making a plant 3 ft. (1 m) high and wide. It needs cool conditions and at least partial shade to produce those sapphire-blue flowers.

Iris
Native to western North America
Zones vary by species
Growth habit Group 7, Tall, clumping

Like most gardeners, I usually associate irises with sunny conditions, but there are a few types which relish light shade. In wetter climates, however, I think they will flower better in full sun if given a cool root run.

The Pacific Coast hybrids (zone 7), derived mostly from *Iris innominata* and *I. douglasiana* (both native to California and Oregon), are a range of easily grown semi-evergreen perennials with dark green narrow leaves making dense clumps 18–24 in. (45–60 cm) high in my conditions. The large flowers, varying in colour from purple through yellow and pink to white, are nearly always beautifully veined and are held just above the leaves in late spring and early summer. They are best divided just after flowering and can grow in full sun or partial shade. Watch out for vole or gopher damage, as these pests can cause considerable damage before being noticed, especially during the winter months (you can protect rhizomes by planting them in chicken wire or other cages). Other Pacific Coast irises, such as *I. bracteata*, *I. fernaldii* and *I. hartwegii* are, as is so often the case, more refined in flower form but are generally a little trickier to grow. Those I have grown are smaller than the hybrids, with grassier leaves and are better associated with plants of smaller stature.

Iris ×*versicolor* 'Mysterious Monique'

Jeffersonia dubia

Even smaller are a group of iris typified by *Iris cristata* (zone 3), which needs humus-rich soil in light shade. This is deciduous and spreads slowly by rhizomes and only grows 6 in. (15 cm) tall, so should be placed with other low-growing plants. The relatively large flowers, about 2 in. (5 cm) across, are produced on 2-in. (5-cm) stems in late spring before the broad leaves fully develop. They can be lilac or purple but in the form 'Alba' are white. *Iris gracilipes* (zone 5) is of similar height but has narrower grassy leaves, forms a tighter clump and has smaller blue and white flowers.

Altogether bigger and nearly bomb-proof is *Iris foetidissima* (zone 6). This is an evergreen with broad grassy leaves that I can only recommend for extensive woodland planting because it will self-seed and the clumps that quickly develop will soon smother smaller neighbours. However, it does have merit, especially in midwinter when its clumps of 24- to 30-in. (60- to 75-cm) foliage still look fresh, setting off the bright orange-red seeds in their drooping seed pods. *Iris foetidissima* 'Variegata' is much better behaved, growing more slowly than you might wish. It very rarely flowers but as a foliage plant its silver-white variegation is as clean and bright as any that can be found for a semi-shaded spot.

Most of the iris that are happy in a water garden will flower better with good light, but provided some sunlight reaches them, *Iris* ×*versicolor* is worth trying in moisture-retentive soils. This species and *I. laevigata* are perfectly at home growing in shallow water, but we have grown the variety 'Mysterious Monique' for many years away from water in partially shaded sites. When in flower, it is always one of the most talked-about plants in the garden.

Jeffersonia dubia

twinleaf
Native to eastern Asia
Zone 5
Growth habit Group 3, Tightly clumping

Twinleaf is a beautiful woodlander that needs well-drained leafy soil in shade. The large pale lavender flowers appear just before the purple-flushed leaves fully expand creating a wonderfully cool combination if the timing of the two does overlap. Later the rounded leaves turn green and are suspended like little parasols over a neat clump. There is a superlative white-flowered form, *Jeffersonia dubia* 'Alba' which lacks the purple-flushed foliage.

Lamprocapnos spectabilis

bleeding heart
Native to China and Korea
Zone 3
Growth habit Group 1, Upright, then arching

This apparently is what we now must call that old cottage garden favourite, *Dicentra spectabilis*, the bleeding heart or "lady in the bath". When grown in cool, humus-rich soil in partial shade there are few perennial plants that can match it. In late spring and early summer the arching pink-flushed 2-ft. (60-cm) stems drip their red-pink heart-shaped lockets amid fresh green dissected foliage. There is a much-loved pure white flowered form, 'Alba', which lacks the pink stems of the species, as well as a golden-leaved variety, 'Gold Heart'.

Lamprocapnos spectabilis 'Gold Heart'

This has the pink-red flowers of the species as well as the pink-flushed stems and is a wonderful plant for brightening a shady corner where the soil is not too dry. The only problem with all the bleeding hearts is that they die down soon after flowering and this can leave a noticeable gap for later in the season. I have planted mine alongside some taller astilbes whose bronzed young foliage complements the bleeding heart when it is in flower and later fills much of its vacated space when the astilbe's leaves fully develop. *Thalictrum delavayi* or some of the later flowering actaeas would do the job equally well.

Leiophyllum buxifolium 'Prostratum'
dwarf sandmyrtle
Native to eastern United States
Zone 5
Growth habit Group 3, Tightly clumping

It's always worthwhile in any small her-baceous bed to have a few choice plants that are visible year-round, and this tiny shrublet is of the right scale to mix with other little gems. It very slowly creates a mounded dome 6–8 in. (15–20 cm) high, with tiny rounded leaves that become smothered in early summer with equally tiny starry white flowers.

Linnaea borealis
twinflower
Native to woodlands of the
    northern hemisphere
Zone 3
Growth habit Group 4, Prostrate

This evergreen shrub creeps along the ground with thread-like reddish stems. It prefers cool, moist situations similar to those found in its natural habitat of

Linnea borealis

pinelands or cold bogs. Blooming in early summer, the many flowers appear as twin pink bells held aloft on short side shoots. The tiny rounded leaves are on a scale to happily combine with other small plants but twinflower is capable of covering quite a large space, so a little thought is needed before introducing it.

Lysimachia
loosestrife, creeping Jenny
Native to North America,
    Europe and eastern Asia
Zones vary by species
Growth habit Group 4, Prostrate
    (*L. nummularia*), and Group
    7, Tall, clumping

Lysimachia nummularia 'Aurea'

Although generally recommended for damp soils, all the lysimachias I have tried have been perfectly at home in any position. There are species, like *Lysimachia punctata* and *L. ciliata* (both zone 4) including the purple-leaved variety 'Firecracker', that I can only recommend for large-scale planting as they are vigorous spreaders, although they would be happy in a semi-shady spot provided the soil is not dry. Of similar size to these at about 3 ft. (1 m) is *L. clethroides* (zone 3). This still spreads but not so frighteningly fast and has terminal arching racemes of white flowers in late summer. It too is happy in the partial shade of a woodland garden where its form and quiet colour seem very much at home.

Spreading vigorously along the ground, the creeping Jenny (*Lysimachia nummularia*) (zone 3), is too vigorous for almost any garden. Its golden-leaved variety 'Aurea' is less vigorous and just about manageable but don't plant it near any special plant or it will soon be smothered. It creates vivid patches of colour, especially when clothed with its bright yellow flowers sprouting from each leaf axil. In shadier spots the yellow foliage will not be as bright nor flowering as extensive. Recently I have planted it to clothe the edges of some ponds and to my surprise have found it is just as happy growing in the water and out into the pond as staying at the margin. In the past I have very successfully used the golden-leaved variety to grow in conjunction with mossy-leaved saxifrages (*Saxifraga ×arendsii*) in a quite sunny site which would normally have been too hot for the saxifrage. Allowing the lysimachia shoots to grow over the saxifrage during the summer months helped prevent the blackbirds from their usual devastating scratching of the latter as well as providing it with shade. At the end of the summer I thin the creeping Jenny shoots to allow more light to reach the saxifrage, which then flowers prolifically the next spring, followed a little later by the lysimachia. Superficially this may appear to be a lot of work, until you factor in the complete lack of weeding necessary for this area due to the density of the plant cover.

Maianthemum oleraceum

Maianthemum

false Solomon's seal
Native to the woodlands of
  eastern North America
Zones vary by species
Growth habit Group 1,
  Upright, then arching

Maianthemum racemosa (zone 3) is the
current botanical name for what we grew
for many years as *Smilacina racemosa*.
Its common name of false Solomon's seal
accurately reflects the look of the plant,
as it does resemble *Polygonatum* species,
but the leaves are much broader and the
flowers held in terminal racemes rather
than appearing from the leaf axils. It is a
valuable and easy plant for the woodland
giving the same structural and textural
qualities to plantings as Solomon's seal
but with a more impressive flowering display. The strongly scented white flowers
are occasionally followed by bunches of
red fruits.

Rarer and also slower to establish in
the garden is *Maianthemum oleraceum*
(zone 5). It has the same basic form as *M.
racemosa* but with fewer, larger flowers in
the racemes and fewer, but longer, arching
purple stems, a combination that produces
a very elegant plant. I have seen a purple-foliaged variety but have not yet been
able to grow it and there are very handsome
forms of this species with lavender-purple
flowers, as yet barely in cultivation.

For many weeks in the spring, *Maianthemum tatsiense* (zone 7) is one of the most
handsome foliage plants in the garden,
when the strong purple-flushed stems
elongate and the leaves unfold. However,
when the flowers eventually appear, it
is a bit of a disappointment. These are
yellow-green and the inflorescence is
too small for the size of the plant but the
yellow-orange fruits that follow partially
make up for its lack of floral impact. Maybe
someone will eventually breed a better
hybrid between this and *M. oleraceum*.

Meconopsis

poppy
Native to western Europe (*M. cambric*)
    and the Himalayas
Zone 7
Growth habit Group 2, Low clumping,
    and Group 7, Tall clumping

The mention of *Meconopsis* to many gardeners immediately conjures images of unbelievably blue large poppies that seem to have been fashioned from crepe paper. These are jaw dropping to the uninitiated and almost unreal even to those who know them, and yet I still cannot bring myself to fall in love with them. I think this is probably because I do not see them as good community plants and therefore have difficulty envisaging suitable companion plants for them. Although they are amazing blooming in late spring and early summer, they do not look good for long periods of the year. I have a similar ambivalence to hybrid tea roses, loving the individual flowers but not the habit and form of the overall plant. These plants just do not fit comfortably in the style of gardening I like to practice.

The perceived wisdom is that *Meconopsis* need heavy feeding to do well, but this in turn means their foliage is lush and their leaves to me are not one of their strengths. In Peter Korn's Swedish garden, he grows blue poppies in pure sand (admittedly with ground water immediately below) and their leaves in these conditions stay close to the ground while the flower stems still rise to 3 ft. (1 m). Not only does this fly in the face of the conventional wisdom of meconopsis being heavy feeders, but it also opens up possibilities of many more companion plants. It ignites in me a glimmer of anticipation that I may still be able to grow the fabled blue poppies as part of a harmonious community of plants.

Most of the blue poppies in cultivation are derived from two species, *Meconopsis betonicifolia* and *M. grandis*, and the hybrids between them, grouped as

Meconopsis ×sheldonii 'Lingholm' and *Corydalis linstowiana*

M. ×sheldonii. The problem in the past was that *M. betonicifolia* tended to be short lived and the best forms of *M. grandis* and *M. sheldonii* though usually perennial, needed to be divided which meant they were always scarce and expensive. A breakthrough came when the normally sterile *M. ×sheldonii* (probably the excellent form 'Slieve Donard') produced some fertile seed. The resulting plants also proved to be fertile, bred true to type and were named 'Lingholm'. There are now quite a few named vegetatively propagated varieties of *M. ×sheldonii* which should all be good. If you want to plant a lot of them and your pockets are not especially deep then you will probably have to raise them from seed and in this case 'Lingholm' would be the best choice.

The other colours of meconopsis flowers are white, red or yellow. Some are monocarpic (which means they die after flowering) which at this stage in my gardening life, unless they self-seed, rules them out of my garden. The reds come into this category. The tall *Meconopsis nepaulensis* can be anything from red through pink to yellow and white and its overwintering rosette of leaves prior to flowering is extremely handsome, but it is monocarpic. More recent to cultivation is the dazzlingly scarlet biennial *M. punicea*. This too is generally monocarpic, perhaps as a result of the drooping flowers (evolved to shed water) being too difficult for pollinating bees to access, although there is a perennial form in cultivation called 'Sichuan Silk'. As it typically requires hand pollination to set seed, I hope more perennial forms emerge because this 2-ft.-tall (60 cm) poppy clearly has the potential to create startling pools of brilliant colour in the woodland garden.

Among the yellow meconopsis there are also a number of monocarpic species but both of the next two mentioned are perennial. I have a very soft spot for the taller of the two, *Meconopsis chelidoniifolia*, which grows to 3 ft. (1 m) in a cool, semi-shady spot with branching, wiry black stems terminated by small, nodding yellow flowers. It overwinters as swollen buds at soil level and dislikes hot, dry summers. If you find the right spot for it, the plant will form clumps quite quickly and adds a graceful

airiness to its corner of the woodland garden. By contrast the Welsh poppy, *M. cambrica*, could not be easier, self-seeding prolifically if allowed to. Growing about 18 in. (45 cm) tall, with fresh green divided leaves and a nearly constant succession of bright yellow or orange flowers it has a lot going for it but the self-seeding can be a problem if you plant it near choice neighbours. For wilder areas, among taller perennials or under trees and shrubs the Welsh poppy can be very effective. There is a very nice single orange-red variety, 'Frances Perry', but I am not keen on any of the double-flowered forms.

Mertensia virginica
Virginia bluebell
Native to eastern United States
Zone 3
Growth habit Group 2, Low clumping

This is a very good perennial for a cool woodland border, growing to about 18 in. (45 cm) high. When they first emerge, the leaves and stems are tinged with purple, which makes a lovely contrast in early spring with the pale yellow wood anemone

Mertensia virginica

Omphalodes cappadocica

Anemone ×lipsiensis 'Pallida'. As the stems elongate, the leaves become more glaucous blue and are later topped by loose sprays of good blue tubular flowers in late spring, after which it dies back quite quickly. In the Maryland woods where I have seen it growing wild, it formed a major part of the spring flora along with *Dicentra cucullaria, Erythronium americanum, Trillium flexipes* and ferns. There is a less common white form 'Alba' in cultivation and I saw a good clean pink-flowered form in the wild, so perhaps that may be introduced one day.

Omphalodes cappadocica
navelwort
Native to woodlands in Turkey
Zone 6
Growth habit Group 5, Low,
   gently spreading

If you like the blue flowers of forget-me-not but don't like the way it rampantly re-seeds, then perhaps this omphalodes will suit you. It's about the same size as forget-me-not, with similar flowers of an equally good blue, but it is reliably perennial in a cool spot in shade or partial shade where it will form slowly spreading clumps and produce a few seedlings. Flowering in spring, it will provide reliable pools of blue making very happy combinations with white or yellow primroses and *Uvularia grandiflora*, without leaving a gap later in the season.

Oresitrophe rupifraga
Native to northeast China
Zone 5
Growth habit Group 2, Low, clumping,
   and Group 6, Bold foliage plants

This plant was recently introduced to cultivation from its native habitat in China, where it inhabits shady rocks and crevices. The panicles of pink flowers on 8-in.

(20-cm) stems appear before the foliage is fully developed. The rounded leaves that follow are up to 1 ft. (30 cm) across and very handsome, held horizontally to form a low mound about 1 ft. (30 cm) high. It appears to be winter hardy and growable outside, but the flowers and young leaves may be vulnerable to late frosts. Plant it in well-drained but moisture-retentive soil with dwarf ferns like adiantums and other low-growing, spring-flowering plants with strong foliage such as *Ourisia, Pachyphragma* and bloodroot (*Sanguinaria*).

Ourisia
Native to the southern hemisphere
Zones vary by species
Growth habit Group 3, Tightly
   clumping evergreen

These are southern hemisphere carpeting plants for cool, slightly moist half-shady spots. The New Zealand mountain foxglove, *Ourisia macrophylla* (zone 9) is a good-looking plant with rosettes of dark green, heavily veined leaves which make a dense carpet 6–8 in. (15–20 cm) high above which in early summer rise the flowering stems carrying several whorls of elegantly held, yellow-tubed, pure white flowers. The hybrid 'Snowflake' also has large white flowers on a dwarfer, more prostrate plant only 2–3 in. (5–7 cm) high. Its leaves are smaller and the flowers are fewer in number so it creates less of a display, but set against this, its size, habit and foliage texture all combine to make it a very useful companion plant in a raised bed filled with similar treasures.

   Ourisia coccinea (zone 7) comes from Chile, with rounded leaves of a fresher green than mountain foxglove, and in its ideal conditions of cool, moisture-retentive soil in partial shade will quickly make spreading mats. The foliage stems creep along the surface, rooting as they go, while the flowering stems rise to about 1 ft. (30

Pachyphragma integrifolium

cm) and are topped by brilliant red, tubular hanging flowers. It is a good companion for adiantums, tiarellas and the smaller hostas.

Pachyphragma integrifolium
Native to the Caucasus mountains
Zone 5
Growth habit Group 2, Low, clumping

This semi-evergreen perennial (the over-wintering leaves are much smaller) from the Caucasus is not particularly flamboyant but is nonetheless a plant of distinction. The rounded, shiny, dark green leaves form a handsome, weed-proof clump 1 ft. (30 cm) high by about 2 ft. (60 cm) wide. It makes a good foil to many of the fresher greens and dissected foliage so prevalent in the spring months. The eye-catching heads of pure white flowers appear in early spring on 1-ft. (30-cm) stems before the leaves fully develop and are like a larger white version of lady's smock (*Cardamine pratensis*). It can very gently seed itself around but in my case, never as much as I would like.

Paeonia
peony
Native to central Asia to
  the Mediterranean
Zones vary by species
Growth habit Group 2, Low, clumping,
  and Group 7, Tall, clumping

Most paeonies love the sun but a few are quite at home in partial shade provided the soil is fertile and reasonably well drained. *Paeonia emodi* (zone 6) from the Himalayas is one such species, growing up to 3 ft. (1 m) high and producing in midspring single white flowers that have a central boss of yellow stamens in branching sprays, making it the first paeony to flower each year in our garden. Like all paeonies, the flowers are fleeting but the emerging leaves and stems of *P. emodi* are flushed with a rich purple and remain this way for several weeks, making a superb contrast to other foliage and flowers of early spring. *Paeonia anomala* (zone 5) from the Ural Mountains to central Asia is similar but smaller at 2 ft. (60 cm) with deep pinkish red flowers.

The Chinese *Paeonia veitchii* (zone 3) will also grow quite happily in light shade, the sort of conditions found at the

Paeonia emodi

Philesia magellanica

Phlox divaricata 'May Breeze'

woodland edge. Growing 18–24 in. (45–60 cm) high and wide, it has good dissected foliage and in spring magenta-pink nodding flowers above the leaves (which are bronzed on emergence). *Paeonia veitchii* var. *woodwardii* is a lower-growing plant at about 1 ft. (30 cm), but is otherwise similar. Both species and variety have excellent but rarely seen white forms.

Philesia magellanica

Native to Chile
Zone 8
Growth habit Group 3, Clumping

Philesia magellanica is another dwarf shrub from the Chilean woodlands. It has dark green, narrow leaves and a tangle of creeping stems that grow 1–2 ft. (30–60 cm) high and eventually spread to 3 ft. (1 m) across. Put it in a moist, shaded spot and your reward for successful cultivation will be the 2-in. (5-cm) bright crimson, trumpet-shaped flowers, like smaller versions of the climber from Chile, *Lapageria rosea*.

Phlox

Native to North America
Zones vary by species
Growth habit Group 4, Prostrate, and
    Group 2, Low, clumping (*P. divaricata*)

The taller perennial phlox are plants for full sun. Those that are suitable for woodland conditions are either prostrate and stem-rooting or low-growing perennials. The first is the Northern phlox, *Phlox adsurgens* (zone 6) from California and Oregon. It forms evergreen mats of interlocking stems 1 ft. (30 cm) across and barely 3 in. (7 cm) high. It has fresh green leaves and terminal clusters of pink flowers marked in the centre with white and darker pink. The cultivar 'Red Buttes' has dark

Podophyllum delavayi

Podophyllum delavayi

blue, almost white) are highly scented while others like 'Chattahoochee' (lavender with a red-purple eye) are much less so. All are lovely but are martyrs to slug attacks in our garden.

Slugs however are not a problem with *Phlox stolonifera* (zone 5). This is the creeping phlox of the Appalachian Mountains, which forms prostrate carpets of fresh green leaves and roots at almost every leaf node. When happy in humus-rich soil in partial shade, creeping phlox forms extensive patches which can be covered in flowers in spring. The flowers can be bright pink in 'Mary Belle Frey', white with paler green leaves in 'Ariane', a lavender-blue in 'Blue Ridge' or rich purple in 'Fran's Purple'. I find them infuriatingly inconsistent, growing beautifully one year (when I love them dearly) then almost dying out the next (when I go off them). The only really consistent *Phlox stolonifera* in my garden is 'Fran's Purple' which reliably looks fabulous growing through the young fronds of the yellow-flowered, bronze-foliaged *Epimedium ecalcaratum* for company.

Podophyllum
custard apple, mayapple
Native to Asia and eastern North America
Zones vary by species
Growth habit Group 6, Bold foliage plants

Podophyllum peltatum (zone 4) is the mayapple, which grows in forests in the eastern half of North America. This species does have a pretty white flower, unfortunately tucked mostly out of sight (as with all podophyllums) beneath the large leaves, but from a gardener's point of view these are primarily foliage plants. Sporting a pair of large broadly rounded leaves atop a relatively long leaf stalk, they create a completely different effect to nearly all other foliage plants.

Podophyllum pleianthum, from Asia (zone 6), has large glossy rounded leaves

pink flowers and broad overlapping petals, while 'Wagon Wheels' has narrower petals of paler pink with darker central stripes.

The wild blue or woodland phlox, *Phlox divaricata* (zone 3), grows in the woods of eastern North America. It is less prostrate, the flowering stems reaching 1 ft. (30 cm) high, with numerous flowers in loose heads. Some cultivars like 'Clouds of Perfume' (powder blue) and 'May Breeze' (very pale

1 ft. (30 cm) across, each with about six to ten shallow lobes on stems 18–24 in. (45–60 cm) high. A clump of these creates an effect much like that of rodgersias. The maroon-red flowers are followed by yellow or red fruits.

The undoubted star of the genus is *Podophyllum delavayi*, from China (zone 6). This too has large, pendulous, maroon-red flowers that hang below the leaves, but it is these leaves which are the real attraction, growing 6–8 in. (15–20 cm) across, being almost unbelievably mottled and marked in shades of red, green and brown, each with a silky sheen when young. It is a fabulous foliage plant growing 12–16 in. (30–40 cm) high for full or partial shade in a cool leafy well-drained soil.

Polygonatum

Solomon's seal
Native to North America, Europe and Asia
Zones vary by species
Growth habit Group 1, Upright, then arching, and Group 5, Very low spreading (*P. graminifolium*)

This family of plants ranges in height from a few inches to 5 ft. (1.5 m), prefers moisture-retentive soils and grows taller in shadier conditions than in full sun. The widely grown Solomon's seal (*Polygonatum* ×*hybridum*, zone 6) is an invaluable plant in a woodland setting. When set among lower-growing plants, it provides a strong structural and textural quality with upright stems which arch over in their tops, horizontally held leaves and pendulous flowers. The only downside of this plant is that the leaves can be eaten by sawfly larvae.

Even better—and almost certainly on my top ten list of spring woodland perennials— is the variety 'Betberg'. From the moment it pushes through the ground in early spring this plant demands attention, with its chocolate-purple stems and unfolding leaves that very gradually fade to olive-green. It

Polygonatum ×*hybridum* 'Betberg' behind *Erythronium* 'Janice'

makes a wonderful contrast to erythroniums and white-flowering *Trillium albidum*.

There is also the variegated *Polygonatum* ×*hybridum* 'Striatum' which is not as striking in the spring as the rarer *P. odoratum* 'Silver Wings' (zone 3). In this the emerging shoots are almost entirely cream, and quickly arch over with a dorsally flattened cobra-like poise. The leaves eventually unfold into the most strongly variegated polygonatum I have seen, and grow to about 2 ft. (60 cm). This is a completely different plant to the silver reversed, green-leaved plant usually sold as 'Silver Wings'.

From the Himalayas, *Polygonatum graminifolium* (zone 3) could hardly be more different. It runs gently underground sending up short stems with purple-flushed grassy leaves from which small rose-purple bells emerge from the leaf axils in midsummer. It grows to a maximum height of only 6 in. (15 cm) and so will clearly be swamped by larger neighbours, so it is a plant for the treasures bed.

Pratia pedunculata

Pratia pedunculata

blue star creeper
Native to New Zealand
Zone 6
Growth habit Group 4, Prostrate

The blue star creeper from New Zealand is even lower growing than the polygonatum in the previous entry, but it is so robust that it is easily able to compete with considerably more vigorous and larger neighbours. It has small ovate leaves, is completely prostrate, and through summer bears a profusion of star-shaped violet-blue flowers. I think it is very pretty, but be warned and do not plant it near smaller plants as it is just too vigorous and very persistent. I have grown it in the past on a north-facing open bank with more vigorous spring bulbs, like some of the erythronium hybrids and *Narcissus cyclamineus* hybrids, which were easily able to grow through the pratia groundcover. It would be equally at home running around under taller perennial plants like *Lamprocapnos* or polygonatums.

Primula

primrose, cowslip
Native worldwide
Zones vary by species
Growth habit Group 2, Low clumping
(generally)

This is a very large and diverse genus with species that require vastly different cultural treatments. Only some primulas are suitable for the dappled shade conditions of woodland beds. Of these, none will thrive in dry soils, some demand very moist or even wet conditions and some are easy and others notoriously difficult to grow.

It seems relevant to start with *Primula vulgaris* (zone 6) native to western and southern Europe, where it seems to prefer to grow on north slopes or the cool side of hedgerows. In our wetter climate of southwest England it is happy to grow nearly anywhere, and very welcome it is too. I won't cover the double varieties of primrose because to do well they need almost annual regular division and replanting. The single named varieties are better able to cope with longer periods of time between division, especially if you mulch them with leafmould or even well-rotted manure. The clean white variety 'Gigha' from the island of that name on the west coast of Scotland is a superb primrose, flowering for months in the spring. *Primula vulgaris* ssp. *sibthorpii* is also reliably perennial, covering itself in the form I grow with lilac-pink flowers with a small yellow eye. Both appear to be self-sterile, at least in my conditions, so division is the only way to increase your stock, but it's well worth doing as repeated groups of these look fabulous dotted among erythroniums, hellebores and wood anemones.

Many of the *Primula ×garryarde* strain of primroses are hardy to zone 4, and have purple-flushed leaves and have been around a long time and most are now difficult to source. *Primula ×garryarde* 'Guinevere' is an exception because it is

Primula vulgaris and *Chionodoxa sardensis*

Primula heloxoda (yellow), *P. bulleyana* (orange) and *Iris sibirica*

quite readily available; it has bronze-purple foliage that makes a wonderful foil for the pale purple-pink flowers, each of which have a small yellow eye. Given a semi-moist soil in partial shade it makes sumptuous clumps of sophisticated spring colour. *Primula* 'Maisie Michael' may well have some *P. ×garryarde* genes because like the species, it has red-purple foliage that serves as a good foil for its rich dark yellow flowers. I am a sucker for these dark-leaved single primroses and none more so than 'Ingram's Blue'. It was bred by Collingwood Ingram in his garden in Kent and predates the seed strains of small-eyed, dark-foliaged primroses known as the cowichans that were very popular thirty years ago, but which seem to have fallen out of favour. 'Ingram's Blue' is a short-stemmed polyanthus type with dark purple-blue flowers and a tiny yellow eye surrounded by a small red margin. A clump of this is as good a dark blue primrose as I have seen.

All primulas that will grow in woodland conditions need cool, moisture-retentive soils but there are sections of the genus that require moist or even wet conditions. These include the candelabra primulas, which have whorls of brightly coloured

flowers on strong flowering stems. If the soil is moist enough, these primulas are happy in full sun but they look well in a woodland setting provided the site is not in complete shade. *Primula bulleyana* (zone 5) is a rich orange candelabra sending up flowering stems to 2 ft. (60 cm), its subspecies *P. beesiana* (zone 5) is slightly smaller, with yellow-eyed flowers of pinkish purple. Grow them together and they are likely to cross, these hybrids imaginatively named *P. ×bulleesiana* (zone 4), with flower colours ranging from yellow to deep purple. The 'Asthore hybrids' are included in this group.

Primula japonica (zone 5) and *P. pulverulenta* (zone 4) are still members of the same section of *Primula* but both are more robust than the previous species. As such they will also grow without wet feet provided the soil is rich and cool enough and they have some shade, but in my experience do better when the soil is damp. The leaves of *P. japonica* are broader (almost cabbagey) and more rugose than most in this group, with flowering stems reaching 32 in. (80 cm). There are named forms with flower colours ranging from deep red, through purple, pale pink to white. *Primula pulverulenta* in rich moist conditions can be even taller—up to 3 ft.

Primula whitei

Primula 'Asthore hybrids'

(1 m)—but is a more refined plant with the flowering stems liberally dusted with white farina and deep pink flowers with an even deeper maroon eye. *Primula pulverulenta* 'Bartley Strain' have the same farina dusting but with flowers of soft rosy pink with a yellow eye, a very beautiful combination.

Reaching 3 ft. (1 m) when happy is *Primula prolifera* (syn. *P. helodoxa*, zone 6). This has whorls of bright yellow flowers on lightly farina-dusted stems and stays in bloom for many weeks. All these candelabra primulas already mentioned will always be happier near water but they have seeded themselves and grow quite happily in the gravel paths in my garden (more an indication of the wetness of my climate than anything else). *Primula secundiflora* (zone 4) is unusual in this section because its flowers are not arranged in the typical multi-whorled candelabra fashion, but arranged in an umbel-like head of drooping, deep crimson, bell-shaped flowers.

The Sikkimensis section contains species with terminal umbels of drooping, sweetly scented flowers and really need damp soil. The more sunny the location, the more moisture they will require at their roots. Their vigorous root systems do not take kindly to being confined in pots so plant them out as soon as you can. *Primula sikkimensis* (zone 5) is the Sikkim cowslip and it can create spectacular displays in the

wild. In cultivation it can grow to 3 ft. (1 m) high. *Primula florindae* (zone 6) is very similar in habit and flower but even bigger, able to reach 4 ft. (1.2 m) when in bloom. Normally yellow flowered, this species can also have red or orange flowers. *Primula alpicola* (zone 4) is the smallest of these three, only growing some 16 in. (40 cm) high, otherwise being superficially similar. However, it does have beautifully scented flowers.

Among smaller primulas that relish damp soil is the very early, shockingly pink *Primula rosea* (zone 4). Despite this strong carmine-pink colour being toned down by the bronzed emerging leaves, it is not easy to blend with other spring flowers, but because it appears so early it is nonetheless welcome. I grew it in a north-facing garden where most of the moisture-loving primulas grew in ordinary soil in partial shade, but attempts to grow *P. rosea* always ended in failure. It never occurred to me that it needed very damp conditions, but now that I know what it needs, it is now thriving at the water's edge at Wildside where it associates really well with calthas, which like the same conditions.

Primula kisoana (zone 4) is a Japanese woodland species which needs full shade. It spreads by underground stolons emerging often at some distance away from the main plant. Each new plant forms a small 6-in.-high (15 cm) clump of hairy, shallow-lobed, kidney-shaped leaves, so it develops into a natural patchwork of plants, ideal for companion planting. The umbels of outward-facing deep rose flowers shine out from the shady conditions where it thrives and are reminiscent of the more commonly grown *P. sieboldii*. There is also a beautiful white-flowered form which is more vigorous even than the species itself. Thriving in dappled shade, *P. sieboldii* (zone 4) itself is ideally suited for deep woodland soils but isn't seen as often as one would expect. It also spreads by underground stems, but makes more distinct clumps with flowers in various shades of purple-pink and white.

My favourite primula section is the Petiolarids, though they are unfortunately not the easiest to grow, especially in hotter and drier conditions. I can only offer a few guidelines from my limited success of growing them in the garden, as there are no hard-and-fast rules. In many cases the summer foliage is replaced in the winter months by a much-reduced rosette of leaves or by a large resting bud, both of which tend to collect water that subsequently freezes and consequently shatters the plant. You must try to keep the plants dry through the winter months while still maintaining as much air movement as possible. Growers try to achieve this in their own ways, some by planting on the leeward side of a sheltering evergreen shrub, others by suspending panes of glass above the plants, and yet others by creating planting sites where the primulas can be planted in a near vertical position. In all cases a nearly fully shaded site is vital, as summer heat is not welcomed, with *Primula whitei* being particularly sensitive if temperatures stay in the high 20s (°C) for more than a week or so. Why bother growing them? Well, to susceptible enthusiasts, a *P. aureata* or *P. whitei* in full-flowering splendour can be hard to resist. *Primula* 'Netta Dennis' is a *P. aureata* cross that seems to be easier to grow; it has less farina on the overwintering leaves but bigger, equally beautiful flowers to the species.

Pteridophyllum racemosum

Pteridophyllum racemosum
Native to Japan
Zone 7
Growth habit Group 3, Tightly clumping

This is a very special Japanese woodlander worthy of the VIP treatment it demands. Forming arching rosettes of dark green pinnate leaves, *Pteridophyllum racemosum* looks for all the world like a small evergreen fern until early summer when it sends up flowering stems to 8 in. (20 cm) with nodding, pure white flowers. It will remain evergreen only if planted in a sheltered spot, and needs a cool, leafmould-rich soil in shade, where hepaticas and dwarf trilliums would also thrive. It is rare and likely to be expensive but it is one of the classiest of woodland aristocrats.

Ramonda

Native to southern Europe
Zone 5
Growth habit Group 3, Tightly
   clumping evergreen

To the uninitiated, ramondas look a bit like the African violet house plant (*Saint-paulia*). *Ramonda myconi* has evergreen rosettes of dark, matt, heavily rugose leaves from the centre of which the flowering stems arise in spring. These stems carry from one to six large, outward-facing flat flowers of lilac-blue, although there are white and pink forms. In the wild it grows on north- and east-facing limestone slopes in the Spanish Pyrenees and this suggests the best way of growing it in the garden—on a cool, sloping site preferably as near vertical as possible to prevent water from gathering and freezing in the plant's crown in winter. The perfect spot is in a north- or east-facing dry stone or retaining wall, where the plant's roots can access the cool soil behind the stones. The more uncommon but otherwise quite similar *R. nathaliae* is a neater plant with clearer blue flowers, and this too has a white-flowered form.

Ranunculus lyallii

Ranunculus

buttercup
Native to worldwide
Zones vary by species
Growth habit Group 5, Low, spreading

This genus includes species many gardeners would much rather not have in the garden, such as creeping buttercup (*Ranunculus repens*) and celandine (*R. ficaria*). Quite possibly the meadow buttercup, *R. acris*, would be included in this list of undesirables as well, except for the pale yellow *R. acris* 'Citrinus' (zone 5) which ought to be more often grown. Much as I welcome *R. ficaria* (zone 4) in a completely natural wood, I do not want it in my garden, but I am happy to plant one or two of its varieties. The purple-leaved 'Coppernob' (orange flowers fading almost white in bright light) and 'Brazen Hussy' (yellow flowered) provide cheery contrasts in early spring to primrose varieties and crocus. It's also hard not to be seduced by the intricacies of the double-flowered 'Collarette'.

Virtually all of the rest of this genus are really plants for full sun but a few look quite at home in the dappled light of woodland conditions. Native to the mountains of central Europe, *Ranunculus aconitifolius* (zone 5) makes a plant about 2 ft. (60 cm) high. In late spring it produces branching heads of single, white buttercup-like flowers. It is a good choice for rich moist soils in partial shade especially in wilder, more natural planting schemes. In the damp meadows of the Swiss Alps I have seen this plant covering vast areas of ground growing with pink *Silene dioica* (pink campion) and yellow *Trollius europaeus* (globeflower), a combination that would work just as well in a lightly shaded woodland. The double-flowered 'Flore Pleno' is a better choice in a more conventional garden setting, with its perfect pompon flowers that last much longer in pristine condition than the single flowers of the species.

Rodgersia pinnata 'Elegans'

Rodgersia pinnata 'Buckland Beauty'

Ranunculus lyallii (zone 6), the mountain buttercup or Mount Cook lily from New Zealand, is one of the largest and most spectacular buttercups in the world, growing up to 3 ft. (1 m) tall. With large dark green, heavily textured rounded leaves and panicles of up to fifteen pristine white flowers that measure 2 in. (5 cm) across and have golden-yellow stamens, this is a very classy buttercup. In its native home it grows in the high light intensity of the mountains but these conditions are difficult to reproduce in the United Kingdom, especially in the south as it also needs a moist atmosphere and a humus-rich soil. The best chance of growing this plant successfully is likely to be in partial shade, perhaps on the banks of a stream where its roots can access moisture. It is worth every effort.

Rodgersia
Native to eastern Asia
Zone 5
Growth habit Group 6, Bold foliage plants

These are large-leaved foliage plants on a scale to match the largest hostas. *Rodgersia aesculifolia* is the only one generally attributed with the chestnut-like leaves its species name implies, but in fact the foliage of most rodgersia species are reminiscent of those of the horse chestnut tree. These perennials like a rich, moisture-retentive but not wet soil and will do well in partial shade or full sun if soil conditions are right. As well as being magnificent foliage plants, many are superb in flower as well, with long branching plumes of tiny pink or white flowers in early summer. Not content with just these attributes, some have richly bronzed young leaves and in others the spent flower spikes (seed heads) are strongly coloured.

Among those with especially good spring foliage are *Rodgersia podophylla* 'Donard selection' and *R*. 'Irish Bronze' (both red-bronze); *R. pinnata* 'Superba', *R*. 'Chocolate Wing' and *R*. 'Perthshire Bronze' (all purple-bronze) and *R*. species Tibet (milk-chocolatey bronze).

For particularly good flowers I recommend *Rodgersia pinnata* 'Buckland Beauty' (darkest pink to almost red); *R. pinnata* 'Superba' (rose pink); *R*. 'Perthshire Bronze' (very large heads of mid-pink from darker buds); and *R*. 'Wildside Salmon' (broad elegant heads of salmon-pink).

For the best-coloured seedheads, choose *Rodgersia pinnata* 'Jade Dragon Mountain' (darkest red) and *R. pinnata* 'Superba' (dark red).

There are other species and now many other named cultivars circulating in gardens, largely as a result of hybridization, and seedling variation arises when the plants

Sanguinaria canadensis

are raised from seed (which is very easy to do). I grow many of them, and there is a wide range of flowerhead shape from narrowly spire-like to broadly triangular, flower colour from white to nearly red and young leaf colour from green through shades of bronze to nearly purple, as well as eventual growth height. They nearly all have merit and when you have raised a number from seed it is hard not to love them all.

Sanguinaria canadensis
bloodroot
Native to North America
Zone 3
Growth habit Group 2, Low, clumping

To see bloodroot flowering in its native habitat such as Maryland woodlands is like seeing little patches of sunshine on the woodland floor. Unfortunately the single form is rather too fleeting in flower although I would still want to grow it for the benefit of its distinctive pale green slightly glaucous scalloped leaves. The beautiful double form *Sanguinaria*

canadensis forma *multiplex* is sterile, so it lasts longer in flower. Propagation is best done by division when the plant is dormant from late summer onwards, but care and gloves are needed as the bloodroot's red sap is toxic.

Saxifraga
saxifrage
Native to the eastern Mediterranean (*S. cymbalaria*), and Japan and China
Zones vary by species
Growth habit, Group 3, Tightly clumping evergreen (*S. cuscutiformis* and *S. fortune*), and Group 4, Prostrate

The vast majority of this large genus are not suitable for woodland conditions. Among those that are I have mentioned the "mossy" saxifrages in conjunction with the golden creeping jenny (*Lysimachia nummularia* 'Aurea'). In spring these are easy evergreens for a reasonably drained cool spot in part shade at the front of the border where they will not be overgrown by taller plants. Even easier to grow is the eastern European

Saxifraga 'Silver Velvet'

biennial *Saxifraga cymbalaria*, which has naturalized in a few places in the United Kingdom. This saxifrage has tiny rounded fresh green leaves forming compact rosettes that stay tight to the ground. Above these in early summer rise sprays of small bright yellow flowers in such numbers as to make a noticeable display. The plants die after flowering but it self-seeds prolifically on any bare soil in partial shade and is really a plant for the wilder woodland garden.

There are a number of spreading, low-growing saxifrages for shady spots. It is best to choose one when it is in flower to be sure what you are getting. Two that are quite similar are *Saxifraga stolonifera* (zone 6) and its botanical variant *S. stolonifera* forma *cuscutiformis* (zone 7). Both have rounded, silver-veined, red-flushed leaves and loose sprays of white flowers, spreading by aerial runners in the same manner as strawberry plants. *Saxifraga cuscutiformis* has more handsome foliage, but is less common and perhaps a little less hardy, although neither are really tough in this respect.

The 'London Pride' group (zone 7) seems to have fallen out of favour in recent years and are not seen as much as they deserve to be. These form loose mats of evergreen, leathery oval leaves (often red flushed below) and sprays of white starry flowers speckled with varying amounts of red. Easy-going carpeting plants like this are very welcome in places—but these are not for areas where your specials are planted.

By contrast the fortunes of *Saxifraga fortunei* and *S. cortusifolia* (both zone 6) seem to be on the rise, and the various forms are well worth a place among the woodland elite. *Saxifraga fortunei* has been planted in gardens for many years. It forms clumps of rounded succulent leaves and airy sprays of white flowers in very late summer and early autumn. In its forms 'Wada's Variety' and 'Rubrifolia' the plants double as handsome foliage specimens as well, 'Wada's Variety' being red flushed on the leaf undersurfaces and 'Rubrifolia' being wholly red flushed. Their habit of self-seeding is a mixed blessing though as the true strains have been diluted over the years, so you should treat these names with a little caution unless choosing the plant yourself. *Saxifraga cortusifolia* var. *rosea* is similar, with fresh green leaves and clean pink flowers earlier in the season. It seems likely this plant has been used in breeding programmes to produce some of the pink-flowered strains now available because there are so many from which to choose. If you grow more than one variety or clone close to each other you will almost certainly have your own hybrids within a couple of years.

Shortia uniflora

Streptopus simplex

Shortia

Native to Japan (*S. galacifolia*)
  and North America
Zone 5
Growth habit Group 3, Tightly
  clumping evergreen

These sub-shrubs from alpine woodlands are among the most beautiful plants we can grow in shady conditions, although they do require special care and attention. Shortias slowly form compact mounds of rounded glossy evergreen leaves which are often red flushed during the winter months. *Shortia uniflora* from Japan has the biggest flowers, especially in the form 'Grandiflora'. The blooms are held singly on short stems above the leaves and are 1-½ in. (3 cm) across, with lightly fringed clean pink or white petals. *Shortia soldanelloides* has similar foliage but different flowers, which are held in drooping clusters with highly fringed petals of bright pink or white. A more vigorous clone with larger leaves is *S. soldanelloides*

var. *magna*. From North America comes *S. galacifolia*, known as oconee bells, a rare woodland plant typically found on stream banks in the southern Appalachians. This American native is similar in foliage to the Japanese species but does not form such compact plants; the flowers are pale pink or white and slightly more funnel-shaped than *S. uniflora*.

Streptopus simplex

twisted-stalk
Zone 7
Native to moist woods and
  scrub in the Himalayas
Growth habit Group 1,
  Upright, then arching

Twisted-stalk is a perennial with a few arching stems growing 2 ft. (60 cm) long, vaguely reminiscent of an elegant disporum or uvularia. A rare plant in our gardens, twisted-stalk deserves to be

Thalictrum delavayi

more widely planted and grown among low-growing treasures where its habit and elegant simplicity can be best appreciated. Emerging alongside the leaves are pendant, solitary, white bell-like flowers, spotted red within, which are much larger than others in this genus, followed by orange-red berries. There are other *Streptopus* species, several native to North America, that I have felt tempted to grow in the past but resisted because of their relatively small flowers.

Thalictrum
meadow rue
Native mainly to northern
    temperate regions
Zone 5
Growth habit Group 7, Tall, clumping

As with many plants in this guide, meadow rue is generally quite happy to grow in full sun in cooler climates provided the soil is moisture retentive, but in hotter and drier gardens, the plant will benefit from partial shade and most species look very much at home in the woodland garden. Nearly all have maidenhair-like foliage and open graceful panicles of fluffy flowers ranging in size from 4 in. (10 cm) to more than 10 ft. (3 m) in height. From my own experience, when grown in the sun the taller species are generally less tall and more compact and conversely more elongated and prone to arching in more shady spots. This is not a disadvantage, because it can imbue them with a degree more elegance denied their more light-privileged counterparts.

Thalictrum delavayi is typical of a whole raft of these taller thalictrums. The lavender-purple sepals and contrasting cream stamens are a recurring colour combination of the flowers of this group. It grows up to 8 ft. (2.5 m) high, with purple-flushed hollow stems supporting hundreds of late-summer flowers on thread-like stalks. Its habit of late emergence in spring means it is a prime candidate for growing among early-flowering spring bulbs like erythroniums, snowdrops and wood anemones. There is a double-flowered form, 'Hewitt's Double', and the white-sepalled 'Album', both lovely but neither an improvement on the species in my opinion.

The flowers of *Thalictrum chelidonii* and *T. rochebrunianum* are similarly coloured to *T. delavayi* but both have larger sepals and larger leaflets. A hybrid of *T. rochebrunianum* with *T. flavum* var. *glaucum* given the name 'Elin', is the tallest thalictrum I have grown reaching nearly 10 ft. (3 m). It has handsome purple-grey foliage and in midsummer it produces masses of cream-stamened, soft rosy pink-lilac flowers. For such a tall plant it is remarkably wind tolerant. Nearly as tall is a more recent sterile hybrid, 'Splendide', with broader petals of lavender-pink giving a bigger splash of colour, even when in bud, than any of the other species mentioned.

The white-flowered 'White Splendide' is equally impressive.

The other parent of *Thalictrum* 'Elin' is *T. flavum* var. *glaucum*. This is a yellow-flowered plant with handsome blue-grey foliage, more tolerant of drier conditions than most thalictrums and growing about 5 ft. (1.5 m) high. Very occasionally offspring from this plant produce yellow-leaved seedlings which are especially bright in their first few weeks of growth in spring. One has been named 'Illuminator' and we named one that arose in our garden 'Buckland'. Both revert to blue-grey foliage by summer.

Flowering in late spring and early summer is *Thalictrum aquilegiifolium*. In this species the leaflets are larger, the foliage forming distinct clumps, both more akin as the specific name suggests to aquilegias. The flowers though are produced in fluffy heads on stems up to 5 ft. (1.5 m) high and can be red-pink through lavender to white. This is an easy species to grow, and it looks just right in the partial shade of the woodland garden.

Coming down in size are those thalictrums which need more careful placement and care. *Thalictrum diffusiflorum* is a challenge for most gardeners, growing with luck to 2–3 ft. (60–90 cm) in height. In appearance it is rather like a smaller-leaved *T. chelidonii*, with frail stems that seem incapable of supporting their own weight. Its redeeming feature is the lilac flowers which are the biggest I have yet encountered in the genus. With luck this feature will be passed on to future hybrids that are more amenable to cultivation.

Easier to grow, clump forming and about 18–24 in. (45–60 cm) in height is *Thalictrum filamentosum*. This has the fluffy flower heads of *T. aquilegiifolium* with the adiantum-like leaves of many of the species. The form I grow has creamy lavender flowers but there are also white forms in cultivation. This thalictrum needs a bit of care in its placement to avoid taller neighbours that might swamp it, but

Tricyrtis macranthopsis

equally must not be put too close to treasured smaller plants which might in turn be swamped. Low-growing epimediums make good companions.

One of the babies of the genus is *Thalictrum kiusianum* which only grows 4 in. (10 cm) high. It spreads slowly by underground stolons and has the usual fluffy, creamy lilac flowers and maidenhair foliage typical of so many other species. It is a treasure in its own right and worthy of a place in a bed of special plants, with cool, humus-rich leafy soil.

Tricyrtis
toad lily
Native to Eastern Asia
Zones vary by species
Growth habit Group 1,
    Upright, then arching

Toad lilies are clump-forming perennials that grow about 18–24 in. (45–60 cm) high and can be planted in shade or partial shade in rich, moist soil. They can very roughly be divided from a gardener's viewpoint into two groups. Those like *Tricyrtis hirta* have upward-facing flowers spotted with red, purple and pink to some extent. This group includes *T. affinis*, *T. stolonifera*, *T. macropoda* and virtually all those with a cultivar name. Also included would be the yellow-flowered *T. latifolia*. All of these are hardy to zone 4, and fairly easy to please if given a cool soil in partial shade.

Trickier to keep looking good are the Japanese yellow-flowered species such as *Tricyrtis flava*, *T. ishiiana*, *T. macrantha*, *T. macranthopsis*, *T. ohsumiensis* and *T. perfoliata* (all hardy to zone 6). Even in the cool climate at Wildside, all these need full shade and a humid atmosphere (an exception is *T. ohsumiensis*, which can tolerate some sun if the roots are kept moist). Most of these species grow in the wild on shady woodland banks where their arching pendulous stems can trail down the slopes.

Unless you can provide similar moist, cool, shady positions the chances are these tricyrtis will show signs of heat stress in the form of yellow or crisped leaves by the time they are due to flower in late summer.

Uvularia
merrybells
Native to North America
Zone 4
Growth habit Group 1,
    Upright, then arching

These are the merrybells of the woods of North America, superficially similar to the disporums but with larger, more showy yellow flowers. All of these uvularias are invaluable as their upright habit and bold foliage provides both a structural and textural element to woodland beds in the same way that disporums, maianthemums

Uvularia perfoliata

Uvularia grandiflora 'Lynda Windsor'

and polygonatums do on a larger scale. Because of their early flowering, the merrybells are a wonderful contrast to other woodland bulbs.

Uvularia grandiflora makes a clump 18–24 in. (45–60 cm) high, with upright arching stems and large, bright yellow, flaring bells in spring. *Uvularia grandiflora* var. *pallida* has slightly smaller flowers of a shade paler colour. The variety 'Lynda Windsor' has pale yellow foliage especially in early spring. All *U. grandiflora* are distinctly clump forming. *Uvularia perfoliata* has straw-yellow flowers which are smaller and the plant has more of a running habit than *U. grandiflora*.

A much rarer plant is *Uvularia carolinianum* 'Variegatum', which has a narrow silver edge to its leaves among which the twinned narrow cream bells do show better. Unlike its cousins, it runs gently, but the stems are more widely spaced, which gives the whole plant a graceful appearance.

Vancouveria
inside-out flower
Native to western North America
Zone 5
Growth habit Group 2, Low, clumping

This genus is closely related to *Epimedium* and really quite similar to it, with attractive dainty foliage and creeping rhizomes that spread quite quickly in the cool leafy soil they prefer. In drier conditions they may spread less quickly, but are best planted away from any small special plants that would likely get engulfed. The flowering stems rise above the carpet of foliage to about 1 ft. (30 cm) and carry sprays of pointed, narrow shuttlecock-shaped flowers in spring. In *Vancouveria hexandra*, also called American barrenwort, these flowers are white and in *V. chrysantha*, the golden inside-out flower, they are yellow.

Vancouveria hexandra

Veratrum

false hellebore, corn lily
Native to damp habitats throughout
the northern hemisphere
Zone 4
Growth habit Group 6, Bold foliage plants

Needing good light and a moist soil, veratrums are plants of the woodland glade or the edge of woodland. I have seen them growing happily in the wild in these conditions as well as in full sun in moist sub-alpine meadows. When the plants are established, the large pleated leaves of the larger species are a prized feature of any garden in the spring and will rival the best hostas at that time (slugs and snails notice the resemblance to hostas as well). These large leaves continue to be produced up the flowering stems to a height of 3–4 ft. (1–1.2 m), giving the effect of a vertical pillar of hosta-like foliage. They make a wonderful planting with other strong foliage plants that like the same conditions such as actaeas, hellebores, hostas, polygonatums and rodgersias, and then perhaps softened with astilbes, ferns and taller epimediums.

Three of the taller veratrums are *Veratrum album*, *V. californicum* and *V. nigrum*. All have similars leaves up to 5–6 ft. (1.5–2 m). They differ in the colour of their flowers, which are held in branching spikes in early summer: *V. album* (greenish white, yellow-green), *V. nigrum* (dark purple-red) and *V. californicum* (white).

As with so many Japanese woodland plants, the *Veratrum* species that come from that part of the world have a certain grace and elegance. *Veratrum maackii* var. *parviflorum* has narrower leaves and more open branching spikes of creamy white. It grows to a similar height as its cousins, to 4 ft. (1.2 m), but it is a more refined plant. The variety 'Japonicum' has red-purple flowers. *Veratrum formosanum* is the baby of the family only reaching 18 in. (45 cm) in height, with narrower leaves and dark red-purple flowers in broad branching spikes.

Veratrum album

In early spring, narcissus and primroses bring some of the first bright colours to the woodland floor.

Bulbs, Corms & Tubers

If trees and shrubs provide the framework for the woodland garden and perennials, grasses and ferns the seasonal furniture, then this section of bulbs, corms and tubers supplies the transient, constantly changing element of surprise. This is a really important group of plants, responsible for some valuable colour in late winter and very early spring, for much of the low-level flower power of the main spring woodland garden and for reinvigorating tired palettes later in the season.

Anything tuberous seems more vulnerable to cold weather when grown in containers than when planted in the ground. I lost every one of over 100 potted *Roscoea purpurea* forma *rubra* 'Red Gurkha' in an unheated polytunnel a few winters back when none were harmed in the garden.

Arisaema
cobra lilies (Asiatic species) or jack-in-the-pulpit (North American species)
Native to Asia and North America
Zones vary by species

This genus of hardy and semi-hardy aroids seems to divide opinion among gardeners. I like them, especially (unfortunately) those of dubious hardiness. I have tried to grow quite a few of these and lost many of them to cold winters while they were still in pots waiting for sites to be ready in the garden. But I am now trying the arisaemas again and this time, until I have enough spare to leave them permanently planted in the garden, I am growing them in meshed aquatic pots that can be plunged into the ground outside through the growing season and then lifted and brought inside for the winter.

One of my favourites, which runs gently underground and soon builds up a large clump, is *Arisaema ciliatum* var. *liubaense* (zone 6). It sends up plentiful elegant hooded spathes striped purple and white.

Arisaema sazensoo

Arisaema kiushianum

When the flowers open at varying heights the effect reminds me of a family group of meercats standing to attention.

Some of the mid-height and taller arisaemas are particularly useful for providing elegant and interesting foliage shapes above low-growing plantings, in the same way a giant of a tree rises above lower species in a tropical forest. *Arisaema consanguineum* (zone 6) falls into this category, although its predominantly green flowers are not very exciting to me, partly because this species carries its flowers under its leaves. However, its form and elegantly fingered foliage is most definitely exciting, especially in its silver-leaved form. *Arisaema nepenthoides* (zone 6) however doesn't hide its flowers, brazenly holding them aloft. Seeing this was one of the highlights of a visit to Heronswood near Seattle, its dark chequered stems rising majestically to 5 ft. (1.5 m), topped with brown and pink spathes. Its elegant form and poise deserve an open situation, and in a less sheltered spot it is unlikely to reach this height.

Another envy-inducing species I encountered in the Pacific Northwest is *Arisaema taiwanense* (zone 7), an arisaema with a fair claim to being one of the best of the whole genus. This has beautiful foliage with distinctive thread-like tips, a handsome dark spathe and gloriously mottled stems. There is also a form with silver-washed leaves.

Three lower-growing species which reach about 2 ft. (60 cm) in height are *Arisaema sikokianum* (zone 5), *A. costatum* and *A. sazensoo* (both zone 6), all of which have handsome dark spathes and good foliage. *Arisaema kiushianum* from Japan only grows about 1 ft. (30 cm) tall and has handsome divided foliage as well as a striped spathe held close to the ground, its tongue-like spadix rising vertically. I grow *A. ringens* (zone 6) less for its flowers than for its bold clump of glossy fresh green leaves which are held in pristine condition until the autumn frosts. It must be placed

Arisaema taiwanense

in in a shady spot, however, as the foliage burns in any direct sunshine.

The clear pink spathes of *Arisaema candidissimum* (zone 5) are striped with white, making it the most instantly recognizable of any arisaema. It grows in nature in sunny sites but seems happy enough in semi-shade, although it may be more free flowering in the sun. The plain green, three-lobed leaves emerge very late, not until early summer at the earliest here at Wildside.

Arum
lord-and-ladies, cuckoo pint
Native to Europe, northern
    Africa and western Asia
Zones vary by species

The European native lords-and-ladies (*Arum maculatum*) will be familiar to many, but is far too vigorous to be introduced into a garden setting. A more well-behaved and refined version is *A. italicum* 'Marmoratum' (zone 5) which has arrow-shaped leaves strikingly veined

Arum 'Chameleon'

Bletilla striata

Bletilla striata
Native to China, Taiwan and Japan
Zone 6

with white. It is a handsome foliage plant which produces its leaves in winter and they remain fresh through the spring. *Arum* 'Chameleon' (zone 7) is similar, but it has larger foliage more heavily splashed in cream and silver. Both flower in the spring with large creamy yellow spathes but I wouldn't call these flowers attractive.

By contrast, the purple autumn flowers of *Arum pictum* (zone 7) are striking to look at, although they are at the mucky end of agricultural in their smell. This arum often grows under pine trees in the Mediterranean where it stays dry through the summer. In northern latitidues, this plant will need more sun and it is not reliably hardy although I have seen it successfully grown under apple trees in a garden orchard. It is a very handsome foliage plant, much more refined than the other species mentioned, with leaves that are more thickly textured and finely lined with silver, especially in the form 'Primrose Warburg'.

I grow this orchid as much for its handsome lance-shaped, rich green foliage reaching 12–18 in. (30–45 cm) high, as for the loose sprays of exotic, slightly scented, magenta flowers that it produces in early to midsummer. The best position for it is in partial shade in a moisture-retentive but well-drained soil. Among other named forms there is a white-flowered *Bletilla striata* var. *alba*, and a thinly white-edged variegated form, *B. striata* 'Albostriata' with purple-pink flowers.

Camassia
camas, quamash
Native to North America
Zone 3

These early-summer flowering bulbs have generally blue starry flowers on upright stems, and range in height. *Camassia quamash* reaches to 18–24 in. (30–45 cm)

Camas and primulas

or taller, *C. leichtlinii* can reach 4 ft. (1.2 m). Both these species are capable of prolific self-seeding so are not really suitable for growing among smaller plants. The small size of *C. quamash* and its rather grassy foliage make it a good choice for growing in grass. The bigger *C. leichtlinii* has correspondingly larger leaves and is one of the few bulbs able and willing to compete with taller perennial plants. Over many years, the two initial colours of white and blue are evolving into a range of different colours from pale pink through to dark purple, with many shades between. The form of *C. quamash* generally encountered in UK gardens has dark blue flowers.

Cardiocrinum
giant lily
Native to the Himalayas
Zone 7

This is by far the largest bulb listed here, capable of reaching 13 ft. (4 m) in height. To reach their full potential, these lilies need rich acid soil in sheltered woodland with plenty of moisture in the growing season.

Cardiocrinum giganteum

The bulbs take several years to reach flowering size (at least seven years from seed) and then they send up flowering stems topped by up to twenty enormous white lilies stained red on their inner surfaces. It is a magnificent sight, and the flowers flood the entire area with their powerfully sweet scent. *Cardiocrinum giganteum* is the largest species, with large soft heart-shaped leaves that slugs adore. I feel they need large trees and a lot of surrounding greenery to give them a stage that does them justice. *Cardiocrinum giganteum* var. *yunnanense* is shorter with purple stems. *Cardiocrinum cordatum* is shorter still, reaching 5 ft. (1.5 m), so it is better suited to smaller-scale settings.

Colchicum

naked ladies
Native to mostly western Asia
   and southern Europe
Zone 5

The common name of this genus refers to the plants' habit of flowering on bare stems in late summer and early autumn before the leaves appear. Colchicums are not normally associated with woodland

Colchicum 'Waterlily'

Colchicum speciosum 'Album'

conditions but are very well suited to the sunnier areas under a light tree canopy. On the north slopes of the Garden House, colchicums were a bit of a disappointment, eagerly anticipated but often flopping over almost as soon as they opened. Never one to write any group of plants off after a less-than-successful first attempt, I tried them again on the sunnier south slopes at Wildside. They must have known it was their last chance, as they have been a revelation. In the bright but dappled light of an orchard, the flower stems stay just that bit shorter and do not collapse as readily under the weight of the large flowers. They are growing well both in the borders along with spring-flowering bulbs and in the thin grass under apple trees. The appearance of these naked ladies is now one of the floral highlights of the entire autumn season.

On the few occasions I have seen colchicums in the wild they were growing on banks free of any other vegetation, their flower stems unsupported by neighbouring plants, and this is the way I prefer to see them in my garden. Counter to what some feel about colchicum foliage, I actually quite like it for much of the year. It does start to get a bit ratty for a week or two in midsummer just before it dies off completely, but for most of the season when growing among spring bulbs its boldness adds strength and contrast to often small-leaved plants in the spring. The broader colchicum leaves

Crocus speciosus 'Albus'

recognizable with its narrow pink petals and pale thin central stripe, and it usually produces enough flowers to make a significant patch of colour. Somewhat more upright in habit but smaller in flower is *C. autumnale* 'Album' which again is surprisingly graceful for a colchicum. Its smaller flowers and foliage are best kept away from the overpowering large-flowered colchicums. Lastly the double flowered lilac-pink variety *C.* 'Waterlily' is worth considering as there is no other colchicum capable of producing such a solid patch of colour.

Crocus

Native to Europe through to western China
Zones vary by species

go well with the stronger, more cabbagey erythronium hybrids and the taller *Narcissus cyclamineus* hybrids, helping to blend the lower-growing woodland perennials into the smaller spring bulbs.

To my untrained eye, many of the numerous hybrids look disconcertingly similar so I tend to stick to those colchicums which are clearly distinct. My season starts in late summer with *Colchicum bivonae*. This has large lightly chequered flowers—and lots of them. Close on its heels comes *C.* 'Nancy Lindsay', the most elegant of the hybrids that I grow, somewhat reminiscent of a large crocus with its narrow fluted outline. In the main flush of colchicum flowering, *C. speciosum* stands out as the shapeliest of the larger flowering forms, where it scales high levels of beauty in the white *C. speciosum* 'Album' and the dark pink 'Atrorubens' which has even darker stems. Not only are they beautiful in their own right, both these varieties add distinct colour variation that enlivens larger plantings of less pricey colchicums such as 'Violet Queen' and 'The Giant'.

Among the smaller-flowered colchicums, *Colchicum laetum* is very

I have yet to see a crocus I could not love (although admittedly one or two of the large hybrids might stretch my loyalty) as they represent the very essence and joy of spring sunshine. A spring woodland garden without any crocus would feel incomplete, yet this is a genus that clearly needs at least some sun for the flowers

Crocus 'Blue Pearl'

to properly open. Most of the species are spring flowering but there are a number that flower in the autumn months, and of these a few are happy in the woodland fraternity in light shade.

Some species, such as the early-flowering *Crocus tommasinianus* (zone 3) seem perfectly well matched to a spring woodland garden. I love it and welcome its prolific self-seeding (although I make sure I don't plant it anywhere near beds containing small treasures). If you want a crocus to give the effect of this species without its

Cyclamen repandum

propensity for taking over your garden then *C.* 'Vanguard' will fit the bill. It has slightly larger flowers and opens as *C. tommasinianus* is starting to fade.

Smaller, and almost as early as the "tommies", *Crocus gargaricus* (zone 6) spreads by underground stolons and has flowers of a glowing bright orange. In moisture-retentive leafy soil in a spot where late-winter sunshine can penetrate, this little crocus lights up the ground. In such a position it will rarely grow to more than 2 in. (5 cm) high, so I combine it with similarly diminutive snowdrops like 'Barbara's Double', very early tuberous corydalis like *Corydalis henrikii* and slender *Iris reticulata* varieties such as 'Pauline' whose purple colour sings with the orange of the crocus. The scale of the various plants in such a woodland vignette has to be carefully matched. In this case the very narrow petals and slender form of the iris works well to my eye, whereas the similarly sized but chunkier *Iris* 'Katharine Hodgkin' does not, lovely though it is.

The commonest of the autumn crocus is *Crocus speciosus* (zone 4), an easy-going species with large flowers. I have seen this species creating a dazzling display of shades of lilac-blue, growing in grass under the shade of several large orchard-like trees showing how it can thrive in light woodland conditions. The white form, *C. speciosus* 'Albus', is particularly pristine

The autumn-flowering *Crocus nudiflorus* (zone 5) seems to prefer a moist woodsy soil in partial shade. This too can create sizeable patches and naturalize in short grass, as has happened at the RHS gardens at Wisley. But perhaps my favourite autumn crocus is *C. banaticus* (zone 6), which has only three outer petals and three smaller upstanding inner petals which make the flower look rather iris-like. It is best grown in cool, moist conditions. There is a very beautiful but unfortunately rare white variety called 'Snowdrift'.

Cyclamen

Native to southern Europe
Zones vary by species

There is something beguiling about any healthy cyclamen species in flower, and many have handsome leaves as well. Any gardener lucky enough to have a sizeable colony of these bulbs should count their blessings. The species most often met in gardens is *Cyclamen hederifolium* (zone 5). As suggested in the species name, the leaf shape is typically ivy-like, usually splashed with varying amounts of silver, but in some sagittate forms the leaves are stretched into elongated arrowhead shapes and their size can vary widely. The biggest leaves and healthiest specimens I have seen have always been on alkaline soils and they can be very long lived. As a teenager, I planted this species on the first rockery I ever made (now in my brother's garden) and was staggered not long ago to see how huge the same plants had grown, with truly enormous leaves.

There are silver-leaved varieties, 'Silver Cloud' and 'White Cloud', and some like 'Bowles' Apollo' with beautifully marbled foliage. The flowers can be pink, white or nearly red, as in the variety 'Ruby Glow'. Of all the cyclamen, *Cyclamen hederifolium* is the most tolerant of a wide range of growing conditions, even happily thriving in thin grass, flowering with us in late summer through late fall. Like the other cyclamen mentioned here, it prefers a cool leafy soil in at least partial shade.

Cyclamen coum (zone 4) flowers in late winter and early spring with smaller, tubbier flowers in brighter shades of pink, carmine-red or white. It is a wonderful companion plant for later-flowering snowdrops, crocus and early dwarf daffodils. Its leaves are smaller than *C. hederifolium*, usually plain dark green on the upper surface, but there are now many forms with varying patterns of silvering,

Cyclamen hederifolium

Cyclamen repandum ssp. *rhodense* growing under greenhouse bench

Cyclamen repandum

Cypripedium japonicum

Cypripedium guttatum × *C. yatabea*

to nearly all-silver leaves. Given a leafy, open soil with partial shade, this species can make some of the brightest patches of colour to be found in the very early spring woodland garden. I have found the smaller leaves of *C. coum* do not appreciate being buffeted around in a windy site, so it seems to benefit from a winter mulch. The very best mulch would be the dried crisped leaves of overhead oaks, but chipped bark seems to work as well. I have also planted winter-flowering heathers, *Erica carnea* varieties, to provide shelter at ground level for the cyclamen.

Cyclamen repandum (zone 7) is the third of the easier cyclamen species to grow in our gardens although I must admit to not being so successful in getting it established. It is marginally less hardy, more especially in the subspecies, but will make sizeable patches in some gardens. In midspring to late spring, the dark carmine-red flowers appear at the same time as the mainly green leaves. There are subspecies with leaves variously splashed and flecked with silver markings (ssp. *rhodense*), and surprisingly easier in my case to establish is *C. repandum* ssp. *peloponnesiacum* with slightly paler flowers.

Very rarely seen as large clumps in the garden is a cyclamen with the most beautifully scented flowers, *Cyclamen purpurascens* (zone 5). Unlike the other species mentioned, this is an evergreen cyclamen. It flowers mainly from midsummer through to

early autumn but can continue to produce occasional flowers right through the winter if the weather is mild. It must have shade, and given a leafy soil it ought to do well in the open garden but rarely does, preferring to thrive under the greenhouse bench. There is a lovely all silver-leaved variety 'Lake Garda' and a scarce white-flowered form, *C. purpurascens* forma *album*, which is worth seeking out.

If you do have a greenhouse with space under a bench, all cyclamen are worth growing and they are likely to seed themselves. Once you have a few spares, try them outside. You may be surprised which ones survive and even thrive. As I write this in midwinter it is probably tempting fate for a prolonged late-winter cold snap by saying that *Cyclamen graecum*, *C. libanoticum* and *C. pseudibericum* (all zone 7, if dry in winter) have survived several winters here outside and have seeded themselves, growing on banks under a sizeable yew tree.

Cypripedium
ladyslipper orchid
**Native to temperate regions of
   the northern hemisphere**
Zones vary by species

The ladyslippers are a source of immense pride and satisfaction for those lucky enough to grow them well. They need partial shade and very well-drained, open soil with plentiful leafmould and generally more alkaline conditions. Their biggest problem I have found in growing them is the damage caused by late frosts to the orchid's early emerging young growth. Some species, such as *Cypripedium japonicum* (zone 5), are more prone to this than later-emerging species such as *C. kentuckiense* (zone 4) and *C. reginae* (zone 2) or *C. ventricosum* (zone 3). They are all supremely beautiful, if slightly comical with their often oversized pouched flowers reminiscent of clown's shoes. All are worth growing, as are the many hybrids which are now finding their way into nurseries. Many of these hybrids such as 'Gisela' and 'Ulla Silkens' are reportedly much easier to grow in the garden, but they are still relatively expensive so don't try them unless you have had success with some of the easier species or hybrids first.

Elegance and *Cypripedium* are not two words that usually go together in my head but there are two Alaskan species which have been crossed to produce just that combination. Seeing *Cypripedium guttatum* × *C. yatabeanum* (zone 2) in its full glory was one of the highlights of a trip to Gothenburg Botanical Garden.

Dactylorhiza

marsh orchid, spotted orchid
Native to Europe and the temperate northern hemishere
Zones vary by species

These are are by far the easiest and most spectacular orchids to establish. The treasures bed is the best place to grow them at first so that you can build up your stock before moving some plants into the garden, where they are more than capable of holding their own. Each year, the plants that are growing well will double in number as two new tubers are produced on either side of a flowering shoot. The best time for dividing these will be immediately after flowering.

The two most flamboyant species are *Dactylorhiza foliosa* (zone 7) and *D. elata* (zone 6). *Dactylorhiza foliosa* is from Madeira, and is surprisingly hardy considering its provenance. It is one of the most colourful orchids that can be grown in the woodland garden. The dense spikes of bright rose-purple flowers can reach 2–2.5 ft. (60–80 cm) in height, with relatively broad, unspotted leaves. Often confused with the Madeiran orchid is *D. elata* from southern

Dactylorhiza ×*grandis* 'Blackthorn Strain'

Dactylorhiza foliosa

from what they considered at the time to be the best naturally occurring seedling in their garden. This was given the name *D. ×grandis* 'Blackthorn Strain' and in good growing conditions can reach nearly 3 ft. (1 m) tall. It has now multiplied into hundreds of plants and is a major feature of the garden here in early summer. Another hybrid that grows well in the garden is *D. ×braunii* (*D. fuchsii* crossed with *D. majalis*) which is shorter with more rose-pink flowers. Occasionally hybrid white seedlings occur and 'Eskimo Nell' is one such very beautiful plant.

Europe. This is of similar size with flowers that are more violet-purple and slightly narrower, sometimes spotted leaves.

Dactylorhiza fuchsii (zone 5) is the European common spotted orchid which grows on neutral and alkaline soils. Its place on acidic soils is taken by the very similar heath spotted orchid, *D. maculata*. Both are very pretty growing in short turf but are completely eclipsed by the hybrids of *D. maculata* with the southern marsh orchid, *D. praetemissa*, which produced *D. ×grandis*. Those I grow at Wildside all originate from a single tuber given to us by friends

Epigaea
Native to the Black Sea region, North America and Japan
Zones vary by species and variety

Epigaea gaultheriodes (zone 7) from the Caucasus area is a low-growing shrub with thick leathery leaves and by far the biggest flowers in the genus. They are a beautiful soft pink, and nearly 2 in. (5 cm) across. It is definitely not easy to grow and needs a sheltered, shady site with acid soil. Somewhat easier are two other species, *E. repens* (zone 3) and *E. asiatica* (zone 4), both with much smaller flowers. *Epigaea repens* is the trailing arbutus or mayflower from North America, with small clusters of white or pink daphne-like flowers. In *E. asiatica* the pink flowers are more tubular and heather-like.

Epipactis
helleborine
Native to temperate regions of the northern hemisphere
Zone vary by species

The helleborines are a genus of orchids that can be easy to grow but they do need moisture-retentive, free-draining and preferably alkaline soils. They can be slow to settle in, but in the right conditions they will form large colonies. They are not the most flamboyant of orchids, with quite small flowers in muted colours held on stems ranging in height from 8 in. (20 cm) in the British native broad-leafed helleborine (*Epipactis helleborine*, zone 3) up to occasionally 3 ft. (1 m) in the giant helleborine (*E. gigantean*, zone 4). In partial shade they would be a good choice close to a path where the subtleties of the intricate flowers are best seen. The most garden-worthy species are *E. gigantea* (zone 4), *E. palustris, E. royleana* (both zone 6) and *E. veratrifolia* (zone 8) and especially hybrids between them such as 'Sabine' which gains from having some hybrid vigour. A selection of *E. gigantea* was found in the wild in California with purple leaves and has been named 'Serpentine Night' (zone 4). From the moment it emerges in the spring this plant has class and is worthy of a place with your most special woodlanders.

Erythronium
fawn lily, trout lily
Native to northern temperate
regions, mainly North America
Zones vary by species

This is by far my favourite group of plants, combining grace and elegance with fairly accommodating cultural needs. As a general rule, the hybrids are easier to grow in the garden than the species and will provide more solid patches of colour. Those few species that are reasonably easy for gardeners will produce a more naturalistic hazy wash of colour. All of the hybrids and perhaps half of the species are plants of deciduous woodland where good light levels are found in the spring. These are amenable to garden cultivation, but if they are in too much shade they will quickly disappear. I also would not recommend

Epipactis gigantea

Erythronium citrinum × *E. hendersonii*

planting them in herbaceous borders as they do not like having other plants grow directly over them until after they have completely died down. Even then, I try to plant them where nothing covers the ground above their bulbs, as I have lost clumps when summer-seeding annuals have occupied the same space after the erythronium season.

Of the approximately thirty *Erythronium* species worldwide, two-thirds hail from the Pacific coastal and mountainous regions of North America. There, summer rainfall is generally scant and so the erythroniums are used to flowering in spring and then dying back for a period of rest during the summer drought before fall rains kickstart new root growth. The more difficult montane species are adapted to deep snow cover for up to eight months of the year, conditions which are very difficult to replicate in any garden not located in such a climate, so I do not recommend them here, restricting myself to those most gardeners can reasonably expect to succeed in the garden.

Many of these easier species grow in the relatively low coastal range of hills in Oregon and California. *Erythronium revolutum* (zone 5) in particular does not

What do erythroniums want?

Soil. Any fertile soil that is not waterlogged. Good drainage is important for all the species, although *Erythronium revolutum* is less fussy in this respect

Aspect. Full sun in cool, wet climates to partial or even full shade in areas with warm spring temperatures. A spring heatwave will definitely shorten the flowering period. Shade that is too dense may cause poor flowering or even loss of the plants. Most erythroniums happily tolerate breezy sites but persistent winds spoil the display.

Care. The bulbs should be firm; do not buy any that are soft. The best time to plant or divide the bulbs is during the summer before the roots start to develop during early autumn. Look for signs of old root growth halfway up the bulb to check you are planting it the right way up, although making a mistake will not be fatal. Allow at least 2 in. (5 cm) of soil above the bulb. They will pull themselves down to the right depth. Established clumps can be safely lifted in their entirety with soil attached as the plants first emerge above ground in the spring.

need a summer dry rest and is especially well suited to garden conditions. This is the only all-pink-flowered species from North America and when suited can self-seed itself, the seedlings taking four years to reach flowering size. However, no matter how many seedlings germinate, in any established patch of *E. revolutum* you rarely see more than two plants very close to one another. It is almost as if they have all decided to keep each other at a respectful arm's length, rather like a nesting gannet colony all spaced just out of pecking range. *Erythronium revolutum* can vary in flower colour from white (rarely) through pale lavender-pink to a dark red-pink. The foliage also varies, from silver-marbled green leaves to others heavily blotched with brown, and flowering stems from green to red-brown. One of the best strains in cultivation is 'God's Valley Form' which comes true from seed, although if you have many different erythroniums it is inevitable that some hybridization will occasionally occur.

Among the white or creamy yellow species *Erythronium oregonum* (zone 5) is probably the most capable of self-seeding itself to semi-naturalize. Once again there is a lot of natural variation in the wild, from pale butter-yellow flowers with yellow anthers to pale cream flowers with cream anthers (*E. oregonum* ssp. *leucandrum*), both in southern Oregon, to the same with yellow anthers in northern Oregon, and then stretching up to large white flowers with yellow anthers further north up into Canada. This species does seem to be a bit more intolerant of summer wet, at least until it is established. In my wet climate I make sure I grow all these white-cream flowered species on banks where they won't get waterlogged in the summer, but in other gardens in drier parts of the country *E. oregonum* seeds itself quite happily in oak woodlands. All of the *E. oregonum* strains are beautiful, but given a choice of just two I would pick *E. oregonum* ssp. *leucandrum* for its early flowering, beautifully marbled leaves (some of the best in the

Erythronium hendersonii

Erythronium 'Apple Blossom'

genus) and creamy yellow flowers and also the large, white-flowered form from British Colombia, botanically not differentiated from the species, which also has good foliage and strong internal flower marking.

Often confused with *Erythronium oregonum*, is *E. californicum* (zone 5), although you can easily distinguish them by looking at the filaments (the stems supporting the anthers) inside the flower. In *E. oregonum* they are much broader at the base (rather like a frog's leg) and in *E. californicum* they are narrow along their length. Also *E. oregonum* has yellow- or cream-coloured anthers and in *E. californicum* they are white. The commonly grown *E.* 'White Beauty' (zone 3) is likely to be a hybrid of garden origin of *E. californicum*. In its best forms *E. californicum* is one of the very best of all erythronium species but it has been in cultivation for a long time and some of its charm and elegance has been diluted by hybridization and non-selective seeding. However, there are still good forms of garden origin such as 'Californian Bronze'.

Erythronium 'California Bronze'

Erythronium hendersonii (zone 5) is favoured by many erythronium enthusiasts, with its dark purple-red eye, dark anthers and pale lavender-to-carmine petals reminiscent of some of the nomocharis. It's one of the first to flower each year. I have not found it easy to establish in the garden which is sad because it is the one I would love to have in many places for both its individual beauty and its potential for passing on the distinctive colour and elegant disposition of the flowers to hybrids with other species. It grows best both in the wild and in gardens with ample moisture around its bulbs in spring followed by dry conditions through the summer, a combination that is not easy to replicate if you don't naturally have it. This species has naturally crossed with *E. citrinum* in the wild and fortunately the resulting plants are much easier to grow in the garden. The three clones I currently grow of *E. citrinum* crossed with *E. hendersonii* vary in the colour of the eye and anthers, with one very close to the paler forms of *E. hendersonii*. All three willingly clump up and, like all erythroniums which do so, can be lifted and divided. The best time to do this is in summer after the foliage has died away.

Until I had seen *Erythronium citrinum* (zone 6) growing in the wild I had struggled to find the right garden conditions for this species. When I saw it for the first time growing under manzanita bushes in southern Oregon it was bathed in the glorious golden glow of a setting sun and made a deep impression on me. I now grow it on a steep west-facing bank under magnolias replicating those wild conditions and it is self-seeding down the slope, a wonderful reminder of that Oregon evening.

Erythronium helenae (zone 5) is another species that will naturalize under the right conditions. A white-flowered species with a distinctive solid yellow centre to its flowers and a beautiful scent of citrus flowers, in the wild it grows under and between small scrubby trees on hillsides which a guide assured me are "as hot as hell" in summer.

Erythronium hybrids (zone 5)

While it is undoubtedly true that species erythroniums are more refined and graceful, the hybrids have the benefit of being generally easier to grow and multiply in the garden. A typical rate of increase for many hybrid erythroniums might be one bulb increasing to four or five every two years, so clumps build up quite quickly. Were I new to erythroniums and planting some in my garden for the first time I would try first to grow the hybrids and then later with increasing experience try more and more of the species. When I first started gardening there were perhaps only three hybrids to choose from, 'White Beauty' and the pale yellow 'Pagoda' and, almost indistinguishable from it, 'Kondo', all still readily available. Now I grow nearly fifty different hybrids and I am sure there will be many more named over the next few years. It is a slow process (at least ten years) from sowing a seed to building up a large enough stock to have surplus bulbs to spare, so most of these hybrids will always be scarce, worth bearing in mind if you dream of extensive plantings.

White and Cream Flowers

'White Beauty' will be the easiest hybrid to find and has been in cultivation the longest. It would be the ideal type to try first, because if you can grow this one well you should have no problems with others. It is an *Erythronium californicum* hybrid that has become slightly diluted over the years by further hybridization with the same species, but everything under the 'White Beauty' label is a good reliable creamy white and should have a distinctive inner red-brown ring.

'Minehaha' is a superb white erythronium that clumps up quickly and flowers prolifically. The individual flower is bigger than in 'White Beauty' and there are more of them on taller stems, giving the clump a more elegant disposition.

'Jeanette Brickell' is another favourite of mine. The yellow colour of the inner flower centre is also distinctively noticeable on the outside of the flower, grading into green where it joins the flower stem. A very elegant plant with silver-washed leaves, but slower to increase than some.

Erythronium 'Wildside hybrid'

'Apple Blossom' has four or five flowers on each tall stem which turn pink with age. Close to *Erythronium oregonum* but clumps up more quickly and is easier to grow.

'Keith' has one or two white flowers per stem with a red eye on dark red-brown flower stems. It is a seedling of 'Rosalind'.

Most of these whites have green leaves lightly marbled with silver, but 'Wildside hybrid' has the best mottled and marbled foliage in the spring. The flowers on brown stems have a charm and grace close to the species it most resembles, *Erythronium oregonum*. 'Craigton Cream' is very similar.

'Margaret Mathew' is a sister seedling to 'Jeanette Brickell' raised by E. B. Anderson in 1956 but not named until 1978. The flower colour is creamy yellow with a greenish tinge, the petals having a slight but distinctive curl. It is one of the most free-flowering hybrids we grow.

'John Brooks' is one of the first erythroniums we raised and is named after my uncle. It may just be an excellent form of *Erythronium californicum* with superbly silver-mottled leaves in spring, but its habit of rapidly clumping up suggests it has some hybrid blood.

Pink Flowers

Nearly all the pink-flowered hybrids to date have *Erythronium revolutum* as a parent. Because there are at least six different distinct strains of this species in cultivation there can be a lot of variation within these hybrids. Some of them have only single flowers on a stem (infrequently two) whereas others may have four or five per stem (multi-headed), and some flower a month earlier than later ones. The leaves may be heavily blotched with red-brown or only lightly silver washed.

'Rosalind' was one of the first to be named. Raised by us at the Garden House in Devon and named after my wife, it is a cross with 'White Beauty'. It flowers midseason with one or two flowers per stem and has white petals, edged and tipped pink with a red eye.

'Janice' is three weeks earlier and the most free flowering of the pinks. The long downward-pointing section of the crook on the brown-red flowering stems is very distinctive. 'Craigton Covergirl' is similar.

'Winifred Loraine' was raised in Greencombe Gardens by Joan Loraine and named after her mother. It has large very pale lavender-pink flowers with a yellow-red ring in the throat and well-marked leaves.

'Carol Scott' is a Scottish hybrid which has good clean light pink flowers on darker stems.

'Blush' was raised by Gary Dunlop in Northern Ireland and is the palest in colour of this section, as its name suggests. 'Flaire' is very similar.

Erythronium 'John Brooks'

Erythronium 'Rosalind'

Erythronium 'Janice'

Erythronium 'Flaire'

Yellow Flowers

'Pagoda' and 'Kondo' are the two oldest hybrids, both with lemon-yellow flowers. The names also appear to be completely interchangeable. One has more brown in the leaves and a slightly more distinct red ring in the flower centre, but I have not been able to discern which hybrid is which. They are easy to source and grow and I'm happy to have them but they lack the refinement of virtually all the other hybrids.

'Brimstone' has large pale creamy yellow flowers with bronzed marbled leaves.

'Jeannine' and 'Citronella' are both very similar, taking after their *Erythronium tuolomnense* parent in the way they hold their bright yellow flowers aloft.

Erythronium 'Susannah'.

'Sundisc' also has bright yellow flowers with noticeably bronze-brown foliage which considerably enhances its garden value.

The two biggest yellow erythroniums are 'Susannah' and 'Eirene'. When established 'Susannah' can reach 2 ft. (60 cm) in height with up to seven large, bright yellow flowers per stem with leaves that are almost hosta-like. It is a wonderful erythronium whose first flowers open facing upwards a bit like a tulip. 'Eirene' is similar but not quite as big and flowers that are more lemon-yellow.

'Joanna' is a two-tone colour, pink on the reverse of the petals and orange-yellow on their insides. It is very free flowering, quick to increase and, despite its seemingly unpromising colour combination, very pretty. Certainly one of the top six erythronium hybrids for garden effect.

Erythronium hybrid

So my stock is now planted on sunny south-facing banks under tree paeonies and deciduous azaleas, alongside *E. multiscapoideum* (zone 5), another erythronium that gets thoroughly baked in summer in its native environment. Both these erythroniums are also beginning to self-seed.

Two yellow-flowered erythroniums from the western United States seem superficially similar, but *Erythronium grandiflorum* and *E. tuolomnense* (both zone 3) have markedly different distributions in the wild and are similarly diverse in their ease of cultivation. The latter species is restricted to very tiny wild populations, but is an easy garden plant and one of the very few species to readily clump up in cultivation. When flowering well, it is a spectacular sight. Unfortunately the clone in cultivation is an irregular flowerer and does not set seed so I hope more clones will soon be introduced. By contrast the avalanche or glacier lily, *E. grandiflorum*, grows over wide areas of the western states, often in vast numbers, but is not easy in gardens (or at least in my garden) although I do have it beginning to self-seed. There are strains of this species with red, yellow or white anthers each colour variation geographically separate from each other, leaving the botanists divided as to whether or not they are sub-species.

The commonest yellow-flowered erythronium species in cultivation is *Erythronium americanum* (zone 3), which together with the closely related and very similar species *E. umbilicatum* (zone 6) and *E. rostratum* (zone 5) are natives to the eastern United States. *Erythronium americanum* is a stoloniferous species producing patches of handsomely blotched small leaves but (all too often) rarely many flowers. This apparent problem is not limited to domestic gardens as I have seen the species covering acres of ground in Maryland with its leaves and barely a handful of flowers through the whole wood. Yet forty miles to the north another wood had virtually every clump with multiple flower spikes. *Erythronium umbilicatum* is native from West Virginia and North Carolina southwards. It has even more beautiful leaves and has always flowered well with me but unfortunately shown little inclination to clump up or run. In recent years my stock has dwindled away, leaving me wondering whether this species is completely hardy coming as it does from a fairly southern location or just sensitive to adverse early spring weather.

The only European species is *Erythronium dens-canis* (zone 3). Rather like *E. americanum* I find that it does not flower well, with the bulbs splitting all too readily into smaller sizes which produce lovely foliage clumps but few flowers. Some varieties appear to be less prone to this than others with 'Old Aberdeen' being one of the best. There are several named cultivars with flowers ranging from white to purple through various shades of pink. They all have beautifully mottled leaves and suffer from a lack of flowers for me. However, I have seen it flower well in other gardens in the United Kingdom, so there is clearly something about my conditions that does not suit it.

Related to this European species is *Erythronium caucasicum* (from the Middle East, zone 5) and *E. sibiricum* (from Siberia, zone 3), both with handsomely marbled foliage and yellow anthers (*E. dens-canis* has bluish anthers). *Erythronium sibiricum* has rose-purple flowers and is not easy to grow. Plantsman Ian Young in Scotland has experimented with repeatedly raising this and many other species from seed and this is resulting in strains more at home in his climate. If other growers did similarly for their conditions, this pretty species could still become a garden-worthy plant.

Erythronium caucasicum is white flowering, by far the earliest to flower at Wildside and relatively easy to grow. As I write this in the first week of January, *E. caucasicum* is waiting for some sunshine to open its first flowers, and will certainly be finished by mid-March. Clearly this early flowering diminishes the opportunities of seeing it at it very finest as the flowers are often spoilt by winter rains and wind.

Fritillaria
fritillary
Native to northern temperate regions
Zones vary by species

Not normally a genus one would associate with the woodland, but worth mentioning alone for the European native, *Fritillaria meleagris* (zone 4), which will tolerate shade and looks good rising above smaller woodland bulbs. Quite often the rather less dense sward of shady woodland means the seedlings have a better chance of growing, so the rate of increase can often be better than in sunny conditions.

One or two other fritillaries do well in woodland conditions as well. From stony grassy slopes and woods in the Pyrenees comes *Fritillaria pyrenaica* (zone 6), one of the easier "frits" for the open garden, quickly bulking up into good-sized clumps. About the same size as the native UK species, this has superficially rather more sombre flowers, usually of dark purple-red on their outside but tipped in yellow-green

Fritillaria thunbergii

Galanthus 'Straffan'

and gold-chequered inside. There is an uncommon paler, more yellow, form. As with *F. meleagris* it will also grow in grass but flowers a little later.

Recommended for a place in semi-shade where tree or shrub roots soak up excess water are a trio of similar species, *Fritillaria acmopetala*, *F. messanensis* and *F. pontica*. The typical petal colouring of *F. acmopetala* (zone 6) is alternately purple then green. The flowers of *F. pontica* (zone 7) as I have grown it are mostly green with washes of brown-purple around the petal edges. The most striking of this trio, and also the most graceful, is *F. messanensis* (zone 7) with purple and bright green, lightly chequered flowers in the form I grow. As with many fritillaries, the patterning is very variable.

Instantly recognizable is *Fritillaria pallidiflora* (zone 3), which has broad, glaucous leaves and three or four large, pale yellow flowers atop each stem. Had I seen this on the show benches of an alpine show and not known it was a fritillary, I wouldn't have guessed it would be quite happy growing in woodland conditions among erythroniums

and dicentras. It is capable of reaching 20 in. (50 cm), although mine is usually half that height.

Altogether different in habit is *Fritillaria thunbergii* (zone 8) which forms a clump of tall, slender stems with the upper leaves modified into tendrils that will twine around any convenient support. The flowers borne on the upper stems are pale yellow chequered with green. This fritillary is to grow in a partially shaded site.

Galanthus
snowdrop
Native to Europe through to the near East
Zone 3

No woodland garden would be complete without snowdrops. Only time will tell whether the current insatiable demand for them is sustainable, as it is pushing up the price of some snowdrops to almost unbelievable levels. Fortunately the prices for some of the best snowdrops for garden effect won't break the bank as they are well established in cultivation. If I were only able to grow one snowdrop it would be 'S. Arnott' and fortunately it is easy to find. Seeing great drifts of this in a friend's garden from the warmth of their house does make you think that as a landscape snowdrop it takes some beating. 'Atkinsii' is another good snowdrop that shows up well from a distance. It is taller and earlier than 'S. Arnott' and doesn't have such a well-proportioned flower, but this is hardly important unless your pleasure of snowdrops derives mainly from studying details of their upturned faces.

Having said that, snowdrops certainly invite closer inspection. Other single-flowered varieties you will not need a mortgage to pay for are 'Merlin', with almost solid green inner tepals, and 'Magnet', with very long pedicels (flower stalks) from which the flowers tremble in any sort of breeze. Slightly more expensive are 'John Gray' which also has long pedicels but larger flowers of beautiful shape; 'Mrs Macnamara' is tall and early flowering soon after Christmas at Wildside; 'Wendy's Gold' with yellow ovary and markings, has always been strongly coloured for me but I have seen it disappointingly lime-green elsewhere.

Among the doubles, I have always had a soft spot for 'Barbara's Double' and 'Hippolyta', both with perfectly formed inner tepals with rarely an aberrant longer one to spoil the effect, and well-shaped outer ones. Of the two 'Hippolyta' has always grown taller with me, up to about 6 in. (15 cm). In my last garden 'Barbara's Double', at closer to 4 in. (10 cm), was a perfect companion to the equally diminutive, brilliantly orange *Crocus gargaricus*, which flowers at the same time, but I have found the mice and rabbits are making it harder to recreate the same combination in our new garden. There are many other doubles of course, many spoiled to my eye by an imperfect set of inner tepals, but there is no doubt they can be very good in the garden, 'Ophelia' being a good example.

One of the joys of snowdrops is their amenability, equally valuable as small clumps of very few bulbs planted amid other early flowering bulbs such as *Iris reticulata* where their individual form and grace can be appreciated, or if funds allow, planted en masse when the subtleties of differing forms count for less. Once planted you can leave snowdrops alone to clump up, dividing them every three or four years if you want bigger patches or if the clumps become so congested that flowering starts to decrease. One myth that is worth puncturing though is that of "planting in the green". Given a choice, always plant or divide snowdrops during late summer or early fall when the bulbs are dormant and before the roots have started to develop. Planting in the green will work but this practice damages active roots unnecessarily.

Lilium
lily
Native to temperate northern hemisphere
Zones vary by species

Even though the native habitats of many lilies are open and sunny, the majority of these bulbs will be happy growing in light woodland. Much like clematis, they enjoy cool conditions at and below ground level but prefer to have their heads in dappled sunlight. Despite knowing of their preferences in the wild, when I think of lilies I always think of them growing among taller shrubs. Maybe this is partly because their flamboyant flowers and elegant disposition are seen more clearly against a backdrop of foliage rather than a competing medley of other flowers, or for practical reasons such as shelter from strong winds or the shrub roots soaking up excess soil moisture keeping the drainage good for the lily bulbs. In the past I have preferred to grow my lilies away from other competing flowers but I think this probably says more of my lack

Lilium formosanum var. *pricei*

Lilium regale

of ambition in growing them in different situations than in their potential beauty in mixed plantings.

Certainly in my dreams my garden is full of lilies imparting their grace and heavenly scent in midsummer. Most flower from midsummer to late summer with a few species that flower earlier in late spring and early summer, including *Lilium lankongense, L. martagon, L.pyrenaicum* and *L. szovitsianum*. My preference is for late-summer or early- autumn planting, and bulbs received later than this are best potted up to avoid planting them into cold and wet soils as without established roots they will be at risk of rotting. The pots should then be kept overwinter under cover and planted out in the spring.

There are many wonderful books on lilies so I will stick to mentioning those that have grown well for me in the past, starting with the well-known *Lilium regale* (zone 4). Easy to grow and relatively inexpensive to buy, its heavily scented trumpet flowers make it an ideal lily to start with. I don't find the shape of the flower head quite as graceful in the trumpet lilies so I tend to plant it in conjunction with other flowers. Flowers of a similar shape, size and colour are also found on another lily, *L. formosanum* var. *pricei* (zone 5), just 8–12 in. (20–30 cm) high. Large scented flowers on such a small plant can seem incongruous if the plant is grown in isolation, but it is transformed when placed among other low-growing plants that flower at the same time. This lily prefers moist, partial shade and is easily raised from seed, even flowering within a year from sowing under good conditions.

Given that my favourite plants are erythroniums, perhaps it is not surprising then that my favourite lilies are those that have similar flower shapes. Topping the bill in this respect is *Lilium canadense* (zone 2) with red or more usually orange flowers, purple spotted within, gracefully suspended on thin flower stalks and growing 3–5 ft. (1–1.5 m) high. At its best this is quite glorious, but it's not an easy species in the United

Kingdom, perhaps preferring the summer heat of its North American homeland.

A lily that is easy to grow in deciduous woodland, even in thin grass, is the Martagon lily, *Lilium martagon* (zone 3). This is long lived and will self-seed but I think it might prefer alkaline soils as it does so much better in a friend's garden in otherwise seemingly identical conditions. The turkscap flowers, mostly in the purple-pink range, are elegantly deployed on stems about 3 ft. (1 m) high. There are two very notable colour variations, *L. martagon* var. *album* (white) and *L. martagon* var. *cattaniae* (almost black). There is a variety of the latter called 'The Moor', which has amazingly dark glossy petals.

With flowers that are similar in shape and disposition flowers as the Martagon

Lilium canadense

lily is *Lilium lankongense* (zone 5). This spreads by producing small bulbs on the ends of its roots, so it has a wandering habit. The sweetly scented flowers are pale purple-pink, heavily spotted purple on 3-ft. (1-m) stems. It likes a cool leafy soil in partial shade. *Lilium duchartrei* (zone 5) has a similar running habit with scented white flowers spotted purple.

Growing in the wild in forest clearings and along the roadside banks and running underground for some considerable distance is *Lilium nepalense* (zone 7) an extraordinary lily by any standards. The stems are rarely higher than 2–3 ft. (60–90 cm), yet they carry huge pendulous flowers of greeny yellow, centrally blotched with red-purple, like some enormous datura. They are completely out of scale with the rest of the plant. I'm still not sure whether I really like it, but it is undeniably eye catching.

I have a soft spot for all the scented oriental lilies especially those looking most like the golden-rayed lily, *Lilium auratum* (zone 5). With a reputation for being short lived due largely to its susceptibility to virus attack, I was not expecting a group of *L. auratum* var. *platyphyllum* to live very long when I bought some bulbs years ago. I planted them well away from any other lilies (to minimize viral infection) in good soil on the top of a bank among rhododendrons, where they could grow up into the sun, and left them to it. Against the odds they not only survived, they positively flourished with no care whatsoever, producing huge flowers nearly 1 ft. (30 cm) across regularly in late summer for fifteen years. Their scent filled that part of the garden for thirty yards in all directions.

Narcissus
daffodil
Native to Europe, North
   Africa and west Asia
Zones vary by species

Daffodils are another of these plants that are questionable for inclusion in a book on woodlanders. To flower properly they must have some sun but they look so right under the light shade of deciduous trees, growing among hellebores, snowdrops and crocus that it would seem wrong to omit them. In fact, I cannot imagine a spring garden without them whether woodland or otherwise. I personally limit myself to growing the dwarfer hybrids and species because they combine so beautifully with other spring bulbs and die back more gracefully than the taller types. It may be no coincidence that the species I like best are those that are happy growing in partial shade, such as the Lent daffodil (*Narcissus pseudonarcissus*, zone 4) and *N. cyclamineus* (zone 6) and its hybrids. Particular favourites of mine are *N. bulbocodium* (zone 6) and especially in its pale yellow variety, *N. bulbocodium* var. *citrinus*, but they do need some sun for part of the day.

Nomocharis
Native to western China and
   northern India
Zones vary by species

These fabulously beautiful plants are very closely allied to lilies, but like the more difficult members of that genus, they are not easy to grow especially in drier conditions. They are most likely to be successful in cool gardens with high summer rainfall, leafy soils and part shade. Even where they do deign to grow it is best to raise them from seed (flowering after three or four years) on a regular basis as the bulbs cannot be relied on to increase, being more likely to diminish in size over time. You may well wonder why you should bother to grow them, but you only have to look into the faces of their variously spotted, purple-centred and fringed flowers to answer that question. There has been so much hybridization between the various species

Nomocharis pardanthina

Pleione bulbocodiodes

Pleione formosana

that attributing a particular plant to a species is very difficult, if not impossible. I have always grown the variously spotted ones which can loosely be connected to *Nomocharis pardanthina* (zone 6) and it would be a strong candidate my list of personal favourites. There are other species or hybrid groups and all are beautiful and worth growing if you can.

Pleione
windowsill orchid
Native to the Himalayas
Zones vary by species

As you might expect from their common name these orchids are not generally considered hardy but some will succeed in sheltered spots in the garden if kept dry through the winter and planted deeper than is recommended for those grown inside. I have been told of a Dutch grower who has

a vertical bank of peat blocks completely covered in pleiones. He has introduced a watering system to keep the peat blocks moist in summer and can presumably cover the bank to keep it dry in winter when the orchids have lost their leaves and require a dry rest period before growth recommences in early spring.

All the vaguely hardy ones are superficially similar, growing to about 6 in. (15 cm) high. *Pleione formosana* (zone 8) has rose-purple sepals and petals and a trumpet-like lip marked with red, orange or yellow spots. *Pleione bulbocodiodes* (zone 8) is of similar size but lacks the white lip and *P. yunnanensis* (zone 7) is smaller and paler than both the previous species. One of the hardiest species is *P. limprichtii* (zone 7), similar but smaller than *P. bulbocoiodes* and with a whiter lip. I have *P. bulbocodiodes* and *P. formosana* doing well in the garden on shaded banks and given a little winter protection in the form of a dry peat mulch covered with a 2-in. (5-cm) polystyrene insulation board. *Pleione yunnanensis* grows unprotected in the peat beds of the Gothenburg Botanic Garden. Pleiones are all really treasured toys, best enjoyed in isolation rather than in conjunction with other plants, although a low carpet of moss is certainly not detrimental.

Roscoea
Native to the Himalayas and China
Zone 6

There is something exotic looking about roscoeas, members of the ginger family, with their broad strap-shaped leaves and vaguely orchid-like flowers. Unlike orchids, however, roscoeas are not very difficult to please, easy to grow in any humus-rich soil and worth trying. Varying in height from 8 in. (20 cm) to 18 in. (45 cm), they associate really well with any of the smaller clump-forming woodland perennials or smaller ferns. They might also be used doubling up in the same areas where spring bulbs are grown as most of them emerge later in the season and even the early ones don't take up much ground space. I don't think they would work as well with large-foliaged plants which might overpower them. Get a taste for them and you can have a roscoea in flower from midspring through to midautumn, with flower colours ranging from white through yellow to pink and sumptuous purple and terracotta.

Earliest to flower with us is *Roscoea cautleyoides*. This has narrower foliage than the others mentioned with correspondingly smaller flowers that are usually lemon-yellow but more rarely may be pink, purple or white. It is one of the few species that

Roscoea purpurea forma *rubra* 'Red Gurkha'

Roscoea 'Kew Beauty'

reliably spreads by self-seeding, most roscoeas at best increasing by just doubling the number of shoots coming from the tuberous roots. *Roscoea* 'Kew Beauty' is supposed to be a variety of this species but is altogether a more handsome plant, larger in all its parts with flowers of pale yellow I suspect there may be some *R. humeana* in its ancestry. It also doesn't self-seed with me.

Roscoea humeana itself has much broader leaves and generally broader petals. The white *R. humeana* forma *alba* is perhaps the most sought after and without doubt the best white roscoea to date, with large crystalline flowers of good shape. There is a lot of interest in this genus among breeders at present and I would not be surprised to come across a good large white-flowered roscoea with purple leaves in the not too distant future.

Roscoea auriculata is one of the first of the rich purple roscoeas to open here at Wildside. When they first open, the flowers are a sumptuous rich purple but they fade very quickly, particularly in bright light, to a nondescript pale purple, so it is best grown in partial shade. The most readily available

Double *Trillium grandiflorum*

roscoea, *R.* ×*beesiana*, is a hybrid of this species with *R. cautleyoides*. As you might expect from a hybrid between a yellow-flowered plant and a purple one, the flowers of this cross can vary, some forms being pale yellow variously streaked with purple and others displaying considerably more purple on their lower petals. There is also a white-flowered clone (with faint purple flecks) of this cross, *R.* ×*beesiana* 'Monique'. All are good garden plants, growing to 12–18 in. (30–45 cm) high, clumping up rapidly and reliably flowering well. The paler clones work well with *Corydalis flexuosa*.

Another roscoea with two-tone colouration is *Roscoea purpurea* 'Wisley Amethyst', which flowers in midsummer. The white and purple combination is more distinct than in *R.* ×*beesiana* and invariably attracts a lot of attention from visitors to the garden. As with most plants the stronger the light the stronger the colour of the flowers, an exception being *R. auriculata* mentioned above. Grown in shade, this plant actually assumes a beautiful ghostly paleness which I prefer to its darker manifestations.

The second half of summer brings most of the other forms of *Roscoea purpurea* in flower colours ranging from near white to terracotta and dark purple. Some have red-purple stems and some have brown-purple leaves, so there is quite a lot of variation. The most distinct flower colour form is *R. purpurea* forma *rubra* 'Red Gurkha' which produces terracotta red flowers in late summer. This desirable form appears to be self-infertile but hybrids with it are beginning to produce some exciting new plants, the best to date being *R.* 'Royal Purple' with dark purple-red flowers and stems with purple-flushed foliage. There are few purple-foliaged plants of upright form in this size range, flowering at this time of year, so the possibilities for exciting plant combinations to stimulate tiring late-summer palates are significant. Try them with the smaller-leaved hostas, *Begonia evansiana*, *Saxifraga stolonifera* or *S. fortunei* or ferns like the silver-leaved athyriums.

Trillium

wakerobin
Native to North America and Asia
Zones vary by species

This is a woodland genus by any definition of woodland, perhaps more so than any other genus of tuberous and bulbous plants. Most of the species come from North America with a few from eastern Asia, but from either continent their natural home is invariably under the shade of deciduous trees. In this environment they are naturally mulched with fallen leaves and so in the garden they benefit from a moisture-retentive soil without excessive moisture which is soaked up in the wild by the tree roots. In home gardens, trilliums do best in partial shade in a moist leafy soil with plenty of organic matter added. I have also found they are best not planted in a windy spot, as even with perfect conditions below ground their fleshy young growths on newly planted trilliums are very prone to being bruised, wind rocked or at worst snapped off at their base. It may be this is not such an issue with established clumps but trilliums are not generally quick to bulk up and such wind rocking and damage just delays a slow process and turns it into an interminably long one.

Nearly all trilliums, large or small, have the same basic habit of growing upwards initially then arching outwards as their leaves unfurl. This shape, so common to woodland plants, is always best displayed when it is seen emerging from lower-growing neighbours (or no neighbours at all) so the plant's symmetry can be fully appreciated. All trilliums are best divided (very carefully) in leaf when they are actively making new root. The dwarfer species, particularly *T. rivale*, can even be divided when in flower, while those with larger softer aerial growth are best left until later, when the flowers have just faded. You will need to make sure the divisions are carefully watered and shaded afterwards until they settle in.

Trilliums are divided into two groups, those with their flowers on a stalk (pedicel) and those without stalks (sessile).

Trillium chloropetalum

Pedicellate Trilliums

The pedicellate group all have plain green leaves, their only variation from this colour is when some species have purple-flushed young leaves, a hint of which may remain on the underside of the leaf or leaf edge. The best-known species in this group is the North American wakerobin, *Trillium grandiflorum* (zone 5), which is perhaps the most popular of all the species, both in the wild and as a garden plant. It is the provincial emblem of Ontario in Canada as well as the state flower of Ohio and it is not hard to see why it is so cherished when you have seen it carpeting its native deciduous woodlands creating displays as spectacular as any bluebell wood. Unlike bluebells, however, it is not in the least thuggish when grown in the garden and maintains its beauty whether a small plant or a large colony. I love this trillium wherever we grow it, either on its own or in company. It looks especially good emerging through a low carpet of the ochre-bronze young foliage of *Adiantum venustum* through which the purple flowers of a *Phlox stolonifera* trail. In another pairing, the white of the trillium can be echoed by the small, starry, white spires of the prostrate *Maianthemum bifolium* and the taller branching pure white pompom sprays of *Ranunculus aconitifolius* 'Flore Pleno' in attendance in the background. *Trillium grandiflorum* often darkens with age to a pink colour but there is an uncommon but very beautiful variety, *T. grandiflorum* 'Roseum', that unusually opens a good pink and then gradually fades with age. There are also several different double forms of this species, the best perhaps being

'Snowbunting' with flowers reminiscent of a gardenia—unfortunately without the scent. However, I have a job regularly flowering this variety and find the semi-doubles much more amenable in this respect.

Trillium ovatum (zone 5) is native to the western side of North America but is so similar to its eastern cousin that it is often confused with *T. grandiflorum*, which usually flowers later and tends to have broader more overlapping petals than *T. ovatum*. The ageing flowers of *T. ovatum* can darken to an almost psychedelic red-purple colour. Personally I have not found this species so easy to establish. There is a dwarf form, *T. ovatum* forma *hibbersonii*, only 2–3 in. (5–7 cm) high, whose flowers may emerge pink or white, quickly ageing to pink. It really needs to be grown among equally small plants.

The easiest pedicellate white trillium I have found to establish is *Trillium flexipes* (zone 4). This has larger leaves than the previous two species which does slightly diminish the floral impact, but these flowers are held well clear of the leaves and I have found it clumps up faster than most and self-seeds quite readily which gives it a score weighted to plus column. *Trillium simile* differs in having a black ovary (as opposed to white in *T. flexipes*) and in a more shapely white flower but is otherwise quite similar. Its flowers are quite sweet smelling.

By contrast, *Trillium erectum* (zone 4) smells of carrion to attract its pollinators. It is a very widespread trillium showing a lot of natural variation and are typically red-purple but can

Trillium flexipes

Trillium ovatum

be yellow or white, all having a dark ovary. In the white forms we have grown it is therefore very similar to *T. simile*, especially when the plants are young. Once settled in, apart from its unpleasant smell, the differences become more apparent as *T. erectum* is generally smaller in height and flower with narrower, more pointed petals.

Red-purple is also the flower colour of *Trillium sulcatum* (zone 5). This species can appear in its lesser forms to be almost identical to *T. erectum* except the green sepals are sulcate (rolled inwards to create a boat shape) but this is not a foolproof way to identify the species as some of our *T. erectum* are also partially sulcate. However in good forms of *T. sulcatum* the plants and flowers can be substantially larger with broader petals of better shape facing outwards.

Trillium vaseyi (zone 5) has the same flower colour and shape as these better forms of the last species but instead of the flowers being held above the foliage they are bent downwards below the leaves. Of all the trilliums with flowers held below the leaves, this is the most showy one. A position in a raised bed will make it easier to appreciate any of these "shy" trilliums that hide their flowers. *Trillium rugellii* is another of this type with smaller white flowers. It is often available and very amenable to cultivation, bulking up quickly, but I have yet to find a position in my garden where I look more fondly on it.

Trillium ovatum

Although its name may have been changed to *Pseudotrillium rivale*, *Trillium rivale* (zone 5) is a low-growing plant right out of the top drawer. Unusual both for where it grows and for the uniqueness of any silvering of its leaves among the pedicellate trilliums, perhaps it is not so surprising it has been moved to a new genus. I saw this trillium covering entire treeless hillsides in southern Oregon growing in very stoney soils, almost rock rubble, many of them with distinct silver marbling to the leaves, almost more like cyclamen than trilliums. Growing only 6 in. (15 cm) high, it can cover itself with beautifully shaped, relatively large white flowers which may be faintly flecked with red spots or very heavily so in the form 'Purple Heart'. There are also some superlative pink forms, none of which as far as I know has a varietal name as yet, usually simply labelled under the moniker of *T. rivale* "pink" or "pink flowered". The largest specimen I saw was growing in the wild in a water seep, so perhaps many of those on the open mountainsides had access to coolness and water among those rocks. Good drainage and a moisture-retentive leafy soil is what I would aim for in the garden, in a place with other small treasures.

Another small pedicellate trillium is *Trillium pusillum* (zone 5), which grows about 6 in. (15 cm) high. With its narrow leaves atop purple stems it looks quite frail but I have found it to be quite a tough little plant that quickly bulks up. Its narrow petals are purple flushed on their backs. Individually it may not look very exciting but a clump is very pretty.

Sessile Trilliums

These trilliums have no flower stalks and so hold their flowers centrally, looking skywards, in the middle of the leaves which are often beautifully mottled and marbled. Were I restricted to just one red-purple trillium of this group it would have to be *Trillium kurabayashii* (zone 5). This has long been grown in the United Kingdom often under the wrong name of *T. sessile*. It reaches 18 in. (45 cm) high, and has leaves heavily mottled with silver and brown and spicily scented reddish brown-purple flowers in early spring. It is the first trillium to flower in my garden, quickly bulks up and appears to be more tolerant of a windy site than most others. It is easily raised from fresh seed, but be warned, growing trilliums from seed is a slow process, seedlings taking at least five years before they flower. *Trillium chloropetalum* var. *chloropetalum* is really very similar except in the forms we grow the leaves are not so heavily marked. The flowers of this species can be in shades of yellow or red-purple. Its white-flowered form is *T. chloropetalum* var. *giganteum*. Both varieties will grow 2 ft. (60 cm) high when established.

Probably my favourite white sessile species is *Trillium albidum* (zone 6), which has plain green leaves and sweetly scented white flowers, some forms flushed red at the base of the petals. It can vary in size from 8 in.

Trillium luteum

(20 cm; this low-growing form differentiated as *T. parviflorum*) to 2 ft. (60 cm) high. I have seen specimens in the wild with leaves on a single stem being 2 ft. (60 cm) across, so even with just two or three stems, a plant of this stature makes a very impressive focal point. The plants in my garden have not even vaguely approached such size, but they do bulk up quickly and reliably flower well.

In its best forms *Trillium cuneatum* (zone 5) has some of the best-marked leaves in the genus. It has been confused in cultivation with the much rarer *T. sessile*, and to a lesser extent now than in the past with *T. chloropetalum* and *T. kurabayashii*. It differs from the last two species by being generally smaller overall, with heavier-textured leaves and usually shorter, musk-scented maroon flowers. It does have yellow forms in the wild but these are rarely seen in our gardens. There are other very beautifully marked foliage trilliums which are only rarely encountered and are perhaps of dubious hardiness coming from the southern United States, such as *T. maculatum* (zone 5) and *T. decipiens* and *T. underwoodii* (both zone 6). I have grown the first of these but its habit of starting into growth in very early spring makes it vulnerable to later cold snaps, so if you try them, plant in a position where the early morning sun does not trick them into early growth. They are all so good I shall certainly try again. From Alabama comes *T. decumbens* (zone 7), the one trillium I really yearn to grow again. I grew it successfully once many years ago, before I realized how uncommon it was. In effect it is like *T. cuneatum* with almost prostrate stems, the beautifully mottled leaves held close to the ground.

The most commonly encountered yellow sessile trillium is *Trillium luteum* (zone 4). There are certainly two forms of this in cultivation, one with smaller, paler, almost straw-coloured flowers with predominantly silver-splashed leaves that bulks up quite quickly, and a second form with larger, brighter yellow flowers, more brown in the leaves and slower to increase. I was always told the flowers of this species should smell of apples, which the second form certainly does, but other reliable sources suggest they should have a strong sweet citrus scent which the first form does. (All rather confusing for us mere mortals.) The best yellow-flowered trillium at Wildside is probably a form of *T. chloropetalum* var. *chloropetalum* or maybe an exceptionally large *T. luteum*. I mention it to point out that unless you have spent a considerable amount of time studying trilliums in the wild, it is probably not a good idea to ascribe accurate identification to many trilliums—there is just such wide species variation in the wild and much hybridization.

Astelia nivicola 'Red Gem' and ferns make a structural statement in a shaded spot.

Ferns, Grasses & Grass-Like Plants

A woodland garden striving to attain a natural ambience is almost bound to include ferns. Indeed, one skilled and talented gardener I know has planted virtually nothing but ferns in a very beautiful natural woodland and it feels entirely sympathetic to the setting. I have never had the opportunity to use this group of plants in such an expansive manner but I incorporate ferns into mixed plantings, so those that follow are all choices that have worked well this way. I love the textures and often delicate tracery of ferns and over the years have grown a considerable number, but I cannot claim any level of real expertise. We grow and acquire new ones that we hope will be distinct, and the following is a selection of those we have liked best. I have reluctantly omitted the tree ferns as I have never been fortunate enough to garden in a place sheltered or warm enough for them to flourish.

The effect of grasses and grass-like plants in a shady or semi-shady environment is very different from that which can be achieved in a sunny location. The dreamy waving heads of flowering grasses as a major counterfoil to mass flowering of perennials is simply not possible to create in a well-shaded site. Instead, think of grasses mainly as foliage plants to provide variation of texture and form. There are of course grasses which are adapted to semi-shady conditions and produce flowers but they are generally more muted than their counterparts for sunny sites.

Adiantum

maidenhair fern
Native to worldwide
Zones vary by species

If you have room for only one fern in your garden, make it a maidenhair. All the hardy or near-hardy species have the unmistakeable look of the well-known house plant *Adiantum capillus-veneris*, the southern or black maidenhair from the southern United States, which is reputedly hardy to zone 7, but in my experience only survives in the United Kingdom, and then very rarely, in very sheltered spots. *Adiantum pedatum* (zone 3) from North America is the tallest, at 18 in. (45 cm). It forms a dense thicket of wiry black stems over which the fan-like fronds spread out. This species has the strongest architectural shape of the adiantums and as such is best used among lower-growing plants, looking good with epimediums, heucheras or tiarellas, among others.

Very similar in the summer, if perhaps a little less tall is *Adiantum aleuticum* 'Japonicum'. This is most notably different in the spring as the fronds emerge a startling coppery pink colour which they hold for several weeks. *Adiantum aleuticum* 'Miss Sharples' has foliage of pale yellow-green, most strikingly yellow in the spring. I grow this variety in half shade, surrounding the taller, dark green–leaved *Disporum longistylum* 'Green Giant' with the terracotta-flowered *Roscoea purpurea* forma *rubra* 'Red Gurkha' coming up through it later in the season. The spring purple leaves of *Disporum*

Adiantum venustum

Adiantum aleuticum 'Japonicum'

cantoniense 'Night Heron' might be even more dramatic among the foliage of this yellow-leaved maidenhair. The last variety of this species I grow is *A. aleuticum* 'Subpumilum' which only grows 8 in. (20 cm) high to form a tight clump, but in all other respects just a much smaller version of *A. pedatum*. Its small size means I use it along with the smaller spring bulbs and compact low-growing perennials like primroses, heloniopsis and haberleas.

Adiantum venustum (zone 5) from the Himalayas differs from these other species by having a running habit. It forms a carpet of delicate foliage 8–12 in. (20–30 cm) high, beautifully ochre-russet coloured in spring, fresh green all the rest of the summer. This spreading habit means it is best not to plant near smaller compact plants which it will overrun. It looks really good fighting it out with other spreaders like *Phlox stolonifera*, *Maianthemum bifolium* or some of the taller epimediums.

Asplenium scolopendrium
hartstongue fern
Native to Europe
Zone 5

The hartstonge fern is completely different to any other fern in this section, with its broad strap-shaped fronds rather than lacy ones. Common on alkaline soils, it is the fern of my childhood, but is one that has struggled on the acidic soils of my gardening adult life. Too common even for consideration as a garden plant when I was young and unable to grow it well since, I am not in a position to be able to suggest how this might be used other than to say it ought to be a really useful foliage plant with the smaller hostas and other more lacy ferns. That hasn't stopped us trying to grow them and of the many varieties, most with crested and undulate fronds, I have always cherished the golden-leaved variety 'Golden Queen'.

Asplenium scolopendrium

Athyrium
lady fern
Native to worldwide
Zones vary by species

This large genus shares its common name with the British native *Athyrium filix-femina* (zone 4) which with its lacy fresh green fronds is itself a beautiful fern. Many of the athyriums have the classic vaguely shuttlecock shape of a typical woodland fern. The group of ferns under the name *A. filix-femina* 'Plumosum' includes some of

the most beautiful forms of the lady fern reaching its highest levels of laciness in *A. filix-femina* 'Plumosum Druery' with quadripinnate foliage (subdivided four times), a fabulous plant and until very recently still the most expensive plant I have ever bought (over twenty-five years ago I paid a very indulgent £25 for a single plant).

This is also the genus where the silver-leaved ferns are found. The most well known are varieties of the Japanese painted fern, *Athyrium nipponicum* (zone 4), which must be the most colourful fern through the summer months. Most of the varieties have a red-purple rachis with silver-grey leaves variously marked in purple. I haven't found it as easy to establish as other ferns, losing it on several occasions, after which one's enthusiasm for a plant starts to diminish a bit. Its colour though is very striking, but to me it lacks a graceful form especially in brighter light conditions where the fronds stay quite low. I prefer it in shadier conditions where the leaves grow taller. Grow it as colourful basal foliage for something taller and architectural, perhaps surrounding a group of the dwarfer purple-leaved phormiums with the blue-leaved *Hosta* 'Halcyon' or similar.

Other silver-leaved athyriums are taller and more graceful, if a little less flamboyant. Their more natural shape and form allows for using them in more natural plant combinations. I have already suggested their suitability for growing with plants showing red-purple in their foliage or stems, such as roscoeas. Elsewhere in our garden, another Japanese woodland fern, the 3 ft. (1 m) high grey-leaved *Athyrium otophorum* (zone 5) and *A. otophorum* var. *okanum* have combined very effectively with the silver-washed, upright, grassy leaves of *Iris ensata* 'Variegata', both having a secondary colour connection of red-purple in the rachises of the fern and the rich purple flowers of the iris. The most silver-leaved taller fern is *A.* 'Ghost' (zone 4), a hybrid of *A. otophorum* and *A. filix-femina*.

Athyrium 'Ghost'

Blechnum
hard fern
Native worldwide
Zones vary by species

The hard ferns are mostly evergreen species that are invaluable in the woodland garden, two of which could hardly be more different. From New Zealand comes *Blechnum penna-marina* (zone 7) a low-growing carpeting species barely reaching 6 in. (15 cm) in height, with neat dark green fronds which are red-brown in colour when young. It is lovely along shady border edges and despite its small size quite vigorous enough to smother smaller neighbours. *Blechnum chilense* (zone 8) from Brazil and the Falkland Islands is more of a bruiser, growing 24–30 in. (60–75cm) high and capable of covering a lot of ground. The young fronds are bright green, their rachises densely covered in pale brown scales, becoming dark green and arching with maturity. Little will grow in this dense cover so it is a plant for large-scale plantings with equally bold companions such as rodgersias and hostas.

Blechnum penna-marina

The deer fern, *Blechnum spicant* (zone 5), is native to Europe and North America. It is a hardier evergreen than either of the other *Blechnum* species listed here and given a cool, moist, lime-free soil will make a plant about 18 in. (45 cm) high, with narrow dark green, comb-like leaves. A handsome fern, often overlooked as a garden plant.

Davallia mariesii
haresfoot fern, rabbit's foot fern
Native to Japan and eastern Asia
Zone 7

This fern is normally grown as a house plant, but planted in the garden when it became too big to stay inside, it has proved surprisingly hardy, coming through our worst winter in three decades completely uncovered. Planted alongside a large peat block to which it has attached itself, its fine lacy leaves are a beautiful foil for nearly anything. The Plant Delights Nursery in the North Carolina has introduced a hardier form of this species they have called 'Korea Rocks'.

Dryopteris
male fern, buckler fern, wood fern
Native to northern temperate zones
Zones vary by species

This genus is represented in the wild in Britain by the male ferns (*Dryopteris filix-mas*) and buckler ferns (*D. dilatata*) so common in the woods and hedgerows and in North America by the giant wood fern, *D. goldiana*. In gardens, however, it is the species from other parts of the world which are more common, many of them coming from the far east and all hardy to zone 5. One of the most frequently encountered is *D. erythrosora*, the Japanese wood fern, which grows about 2 ft. (60 cm) high. Its most striking feature are the glossy copper-pink young fronds which gradually turn green as they mature and then last well into the winter. I have it happily growing with Bowles' golden grass (*Milium effusum* 'Aureum') producing a nice blend of colours and textures in the spring.

The North American *Dryopteris goldiana* (zone 3) is perhaps most notable for the shaggy white and brown scales on the unfurling fronds, but this feature is taken to another level by a fern from the Himalayas,

Onoclea sensibilis copper-leaved form

D. wallichiana (zone 6). In this the rachis is thickly covered by black scales contrasting with the bright golden green of the young leaves, a contrast which remains in less dramatic fashion through the season as the fronds mature to more conventional green. It is very beautiful, but also slightly sinister.

A fern that impressed me enormously on a visit to Heronswood was *Dryopteris crassirhizoma* (zone 5). This was clearly quite an old specimen as it had built up a sizeable crown above ground from which the wide spreading fronds each stretched to nearly 3 ft. (1 m) long. It gave a wonderfully tropical effect rather like a very short-trunked tree fern.

Matteucia struthiopteris
ostrich fern, shuttlecock fern
Native to northern temperate areas
Zone 2

The ferns in this genus spread by rhizomes and will cover a considerable area in good conditions. With a strongly vase-shaped habit, ostrich fern is particularly handsome as the fronds unfurl. The fresh green

leaves make this a very attractive fern but really only for larger gardens as it is capable of reaching 5-½ ft. (1-½ m) high, although in my gardens it has only grown to half that. The strong architectural shape is very often lost in the mass of crowns but can be made more pronounced if the smaller crowns are removed, leaving space around the larger ones.

Onoclea sensibilis
sensitive fern
Native to Asia and eastern North America
Zone 4

Called the sensitive fern because its fronds wither away when the temperatures drop close to freezing, this *Onoclea* is actually very hardy. It is another species that rapidly spreads by rhizomes, with fronds reaching about 18 in. (45 cm) in height. Despite its propensity to shrivel up at the first sign of frost, it is a very handsome, bold-leaved fern especially in the form simply known as 'copper-leaved' with coppery brown young fronds which retain some of this colour throughout the season around the leaf edges. It will grow in a wide range of conditions and is likely to be less vigorous in drier shade. In damper conditions, the sensitive fern can spread alarmingly and is even able to grow at the edge of a stream or pond, although you would be a brave person to introduce this to any but larger ponds. It is very handsome paired with larger hostas and rodgersias.

Onychium japonicum
Japanese carrot fern
Native to Japan and the far East
Zone 7

The Japanese carrot fern is a very beautiful, very lacy plant, just about hardy throughout the United Kingdom, the Pacific Northest, and the southern United States. It slowly builds up into clumps about 2 ft. (60 cm) high. It is surprisingly resilient when established, in my garden several clumps push up every year through a seemingly

Osmunda lancea

impenetrable carpet of sweet woodruff (*Galium odoratum*) and *Adiantum venustum* which together invaded the taller fern's space. This was a lucky happenstance that resulted in a good combination of textures and greens, but really the classy onychium deserves more care in its placement.

Osmunda

royal fern
Native to northern temperate regions
Zones vary by species

Among this European, African and Asian genus are the royal ferns, which revel in moist or even wet soils. The adjectives *regal* and *majestic* do seem to apply to the large *Osmunda regalis* (zone 3) which can reach 9 ft. (3 m) high in ideal conditions, although it is usually less than half this. It is the perfect fern for waterside planting on any but small ponds. The leaves are large, but broken down into much smaller subdivisions which allows it to be sit alongside smaller-foliaged plants such as irisies or astilbes or—at the other extreme—with that giant of all streamside plants, *Gunnera manicata*. The purple leaved variety *O. regalis* 'Purpurascens' is especially good in the spring with its purple rachises and pink-copper young fronds, which retain a reddish caste even in maturity.

The interrupted fern (*Osmunda claytoniana*, zone 3) is from North America and the Himalayas, gets its common name for the middle section of the fronds which bear the fertile pinnae. It is a handsome deciduous fern for medium to wet soils in part or full shade growing up to 3 ft. (1 m) high.

From Japan, *Osmunda lancea* (zone 6) is by far the rarest in cultivation of those mentioned here. I include it in the hope that increased interest in this most graceful of the osmundas might help to make it become more readily available. The elegant fronds grow up to 2 ft. (60 cm) high and are bronze coloured on emergence. *Osmunda japonica* (zone 6) is similar but taller, growing up to 3 ft. (1 m). In its native Japan, the young fronds are widely enjoyed as a vegetable.

Polystichum

shield fern, sword fern
Native to temperate and tropical
   regions worldwide
Zones vary by species

This is a large genus of mainly evergreen
clump-forming ferns, many with dark
green leaves of which the soft shield fern,
Polystichum setiferum (zone 5), is the most
important. This one species has given
rise to more varieties and selections than
any other British fern, many of which are
still in cultivation. Some are dwarf, like *P.
setiferum* 'Congestum' which grows only
about 6 in. (15 cm) high. Many are crested
where the frond tips and pinnae are further
divided into tassels or crests, a few have
narrow pinnae giving a more lacy effect and
yet others, such as *P. setiferum* Plumo-
sodivisilobum group, have leaves so finely
divided they appear almost moss-like. The
taller ones reach a height of about 3 ft. (1 m)
typically with a wide-spreading vase
shape and are perfect for combining with
all low or medium-sized clump-forming

Polystichum munitum

Bamboo for shade?

This is a group of grasses that I love dearly but which are difficult to incorporate
into a woodland garden because of their generally large size. The form and grace
of the larger-growing types are best appreciated when grown as specimens, but
to incorporate specimens of this magnitude you need a pretty large wood. Failing
this, they are unsurpassed as background or boundary plantings. I prefer to
remove the thinnest canes from the clumps every year as this seems to encourage the development of thicker, more impressive canes showing off those that
remain to better advantage. There are some smaller bamboos under 5 ft. (1.5 m)
high which are much easier to grow in a loose community of plants. The most
striking is *Pleioblastus viridistriatus* (zone 7). I cut this to the ground every spring
and it then grows back up to about 3 ft. (1 m) with bright yellow leaves striped
thinly with green. The foliage on this upright clump remain the brightest splash
of colour in the whole garden through the winter months. Care needs to be
taken with its placement though as it can spread quite quickly when in good soil.

perennials such as dicentras, epimediums and trilliums. One of my favourites of these taller varieties has always been *P. setiferum* 'Pulcherrimum Bevis', once a scarce plant but fortunately now fairly easily sourced. This has graceful fronds of silky texture with elegant tapering tips.

Among the North America natives are two handsome evergreen polystichums ideal for almost any woodland garden that has space for them. These are the Christmas fern, *Polystichum acrostichoides* (zone 3), and the sword fern, *P. munitum* (zone 4). Both are very similar in foliage but *P. munitum* makes a much larger plant forming a tight but gracefully arching clump up to 5 ft. (1.5 m) high.

Polypodium
polypody
Native to eastern Europe and the Pacific Northwest
Zone 5

If you have ever seen ferns growing on tree branches in the wetter parts of the United Kingdom it is almost certainly the common polypody, *Polypodium vulgare*, or the closely related *P. cambricum*. These can also be seen in hedgerows, on walls and mossy rocks, preferring very stony ground and only very rarely grow in good soils. This is relevant because there are a few varieties which are worth growing in our gardens and they likewise prefer better-drained locations. The form *P. cambricum* 'Cambricum' is probably the best with plumose fronds of fresh light green that slowly spread to form mats 8–12 in. (20–30 cm) high. *Polypodium vulgare* 'Cornubiense' is equally feathery but occasionally produces reverted fronds as well which should be removed. Introduced to, and invasive in, New Zealand.

Carex elata 'Aurea'

Astelia nervosa
Native to New Zealand
Zone 8

This is an evergreen clump-forming perennial of montane grasslands and forests. From a distance it looks like a grey-leaved, low-growing phormium with thicker-textured leaves and a more arching habit growing 24–30 in. (60–75 cm) high by about 3 ft. (1 m) wide. Close up, the leaves are longitudinally striped olive green, silver and purple offering the gardener different options for successfully colour blending it with neighbouring plants. There is a dwarfer, more purple-leaved form called 'Westland' (and there are others) which for me lacks some of the charm of the species, so I am content to stick with the simplicity of the "plain" astelia.

Carex
sedge
Native worldwide
Zones vary by species

A huge genus, sedges are found mostly in wet or moist soils. Of those I have seen, while suited to shady conditions in hotter or drier climates than my own, with a few notable exceptions, none have filled me with an overwhelming urge to grow them myself. Flowers are not often their strong point, so the main reason for growing them is as foliage plants.

The sedge I use most is the hair sedge, *Carex comans* (zone 7), which is native to New Zealand and has a domed habit to 18 in. (45 cm) with pendent bronzed foliage. This and other similarly coloured carex, like *C. buchananii* (leatherleaf sedge) and *C. testacea* (orange New Zealand sedge) are both hardy to zone 7 and normally recommended for full-sun situations, but having seen them used to extensively cover ground under trees in a Scottish garden, I have also used

them in shade very successfully. As with other brown- or purple-leaved plants, the trick to avoiding them just looking dead is to surround them with greenery or a mulch of lighter-coloured gravel. I once grew these sedges in a shaded spot undercarpeted with *Pratia pedunculata* which provided a long-lasting carpet of tiny pale blue flowers. In our present garden I have variegated *Daphne odora* emerging above surrounding *C. comans*, the grass providing valuable winter protection as an added bonus. In other places these bronzed carex look good with golden chippings or gravel as a mulch that accentuates both the colour and the domed and weeping habit of the sedge.

Forming dense mats 8 in. (20 cm) high is the relatively broad-leaved *Carex siderosticha* 'Variegata' (zone 6). Needing a moisture-retentive soil and part-shade this is a handsome grass with the leaves edged in white and usually pink-flushed on the new growth in spring. Being deciduous, its only downside is it can be a little untidy in the winter unless you cut it back in the autumn.

Another variegated sedge creating tighter clumps, 1 ft. (30 cm) high, with much narrower foliage is *Carex oshimensis* 'Evergold' (zone 6). This has striking creamy yellow variegation and being evergreen looks good all winter as well. It can form bold combinations with the various-coloured leaves of ophiopogon, liriopes and other dwarf grasses.

Two sedges whose leaves emerge towards the top of 2 ft. (60 cm) stems are the green-leaved palm sedge, *Carex muskingumensis* (zone 4) which can form sizeable colonies in moist soil in partial shade and the more refined but less hardy *C. phyllocephala* 'Sparkler' (zone 8), needing similar conditions, with very striking creamy white variegated foliage. Both are good foliage plants but the vigour of the palm sedge needs watching, whereas the variegated 'Sparkler' is worthy of a good spot in a container.

One of my all-time favourite golden

Chionochloa rubra

grasses is *Carex elata* 'Aurea', Bowles' golden sedge (zone 5). This has the most intense yellow foliage in the spring of any grass I can think of, and unusually for a sedge has attractive flowers at the same time. The best colour will be achieved in full sun, but even in partial shade the leaves are still an attractive lime-yellow colour. It is happy to grow in the border where it reaches about 30 in. (75 cm) in height, it can even be grown in shallow water where its elegant form can be fully appreciated.

Chionochloa rubra
red tussock grass
Native to New Zealand
Zone 8

This is another favourite grass from New Zealand, where it grows on open hillsides. I use it extensively in the sunnier parts of our garden, not for its flowers but mainly for its clumps of evergreen arching thread-like brown-green foliage that reach 3 ft. (1 m) high. Because of this, it also makes a valuable

addition to semi-shady spots in the woodland garden. The foliage colour may not be as intense as in full sun, perhaps being more olive green, but its elegant form and texture make it a perfect specimen grass growing out of smaller lower-growing neighbours.

Hakonechloa macra
Japanese Hakone grass
Native to Japan
Zone 4, except as noted

This may be the finest of all grasses for the woodland garden. *Hakonechloa macra* forms graceful arching clumps, 2–3 ft. (60–90 cm) high, with billowing, cascading rich green leaves topped by sprays of tiny dark flowers in late summer. In autumn the foliage deepens to an ochre-red and continues to look good all winter. Even more impressive is its slightly less hardy golden-variegated form, 'Aureola' (zone 6), easily the most graceful golden-leaved grass that can be grown in partial shade. There are now various variegated forms of this species varying from nearly all gold (rather than striped) to a paler yellow. The colour of all of these variegated forms tends to get a little bleached in sunny sites.

Liriope
lily turf
Native to eastern Asia
Zone 5

These are low-growing, clump-forming evergreen perennials very similar in leaf and size to ophiopogons but more impressive in flower. *Liriope muscari* has green leaves and flowers in autumn with dense 1-ft. (30-cm) spikes of purple-violet flowers (similar to a muscari's flower spike) followed by black berries. They can make quite an impressive display in a shady or part-shady spot. There are several varieties of this species with varying flower colours, some forms are variegated, and clones of different heights, some like 'Big Blue' reaching 18 in. (45 cm) in height.

Milium effusum 'Aureum'
Bowles' golden grass
Native to Europe, northeastern
United States and Japan.
Zone 5

This is another stalwart of the spring woodland garden which brings wonderful patches of bright greeny yellow foliage to the scene. It self-seeds readily at Wildside, the seedlings popping up in unusual but often very welcome places. These are very easily pulled up if not required. Best in partial shade. Growing up to 2 ft. (60 cm) high, it is especially dainty in flower in the company of other plants but can appear a bit "weedy" in isolation.

Hakonechloa macra varieties

Liriope muscari

Yucca flaccida 'Golden Sword'

Milium effusum 'Aureum'

Ophiopogon planiscapus 'Nigrescens'

Ophiopogon
Native to Japan
Zone 6

There are various ophiopogons but the two I have enjoyed growing are noted for their coloured foliage. Both have narrow grassy evergreen leaves and a slowly creeping habit and are only about 6 in. (15 cm) high. Strangely, these plants are in the same family as asparagus and have short spikes of flowers followed by dark blue-purple fruits. *Ophiopogon planiscapus* 'Nigrescens', black lilyturf, has almost black foliage and purple flowers, *Ophiopogon* 'Little Tabby' has green leaves cleanly margined with white and white flowers. Both are happy to grow in full sun or part-shade.

Yucca flaccida 'Golden Sword'
Native to arid regions of North, South, and Central America
Zone 4

This is perhaps a surprising concluding addition to directory of woodland plants, but the variegated *Yucca flaccida* 'Golden Sword' has proved to be remarkably good value in the semi-shade of our garden, flowering well and holding its bright colour in sites with good light levels but where it receives no direct sun at all. As a focal point in a design for woodland plants in a garden close to the house or a building this would be a good choice.

Suggestions for further reading

Case, Frederick W., and Roberta B. Case. *Trilliums*. Timber Press, 2009.

Darke, Rick. *The American Woodland Garden*. Timber Press, 2002.

Elliot, Jack. *The Woodland Garden*. AGS Publications, 1998.

Evans, Alfrend. *The Peat Garden and its Plants*. J. M. Dent & Son, 1974.

> Practical advice on the construction of peat beds and descriptions of many of the choicest woodlanders grown by the late Assistant Curator at the Edinburgh Botanic Garden.

Hinkley, Dan. *The Explorer's Garden*. Timber Press, 1999.

Ian Young's Bulb blog for the Scottish Rock Garden Club. www.srgc.org.uk.

Korn, Peter. *Peter Korns Garden: Giving Plants What They Want*. Self-published.

> Observations on natural plant habitats and growing plants in sand beds.

Tebbitt, Mark C., Magnus Liden and Henrik Zetterlund. *Bleeding Hearts, Corydalis, and Their Relatives*. Timber Press, 2008.

Thomas, Graham Stuart. *Perennial Garden Plants*. J. M. Dent & Son, 2004.

Wiley, Keith. *On the Wild Side*. Timber Press, 2004.

> On taking gardening inspiration from nature.

Wiley, Keith. *Shade*. Timber Press, 2006.

> Contains ideas and inspiration for shady gardens.

Acknowledgements

My principal thanks must go to Robin and Sue White of Blackthorn Nursery for their overwhelmingly generous support, knowledge and advice, and for being simply the best growers of non-woody plants I have ever met. Thanks too to Peter Chappell for his boundless enthusiasm, which has inspired me to see the possibilities of woodland plants in our visits to his wonderful garden at Spinners over many years.

For this book I would like to thank Martin Walsh for his prompt and detailed responses to questions about plants growing in the Himalayas and for allowing me to use some of his wonderful photographs. Thanks also to Barry Starling for sharing over many years his knowledge of plants growing in the wild. For allowing me to use a few of their photographs, thanks are due to Peter Erskine, Ian Christie and Mary Gore, as they are for all those people, too many to mention, who have kindly shown me their gardens and given me warm hospitality. Grateful thanks too for editorial input from Fiona Gilsenan who created some semblance of order from my scattergun ideas.

Lastly and above all, to my wife, Ros, without whose support, hard work, tenacity and particularly patience, none of what is described in this book would have been possible, my eternal gratitude.

Photo credits

Alan Detrick and Linda Detrick: pages 28, 32 top, 116, 128, 131, 134 right, 140 left, 164 right, 199 top, 208 top left

Ian Christie: page 150

iStock Photo: pages 13, 17 top, 24 top, 30 top, 43, 49 top, 82, 108 bottom, 143 left, 152, 155

Lynne Harrison: pages 42 top, 87 bottom, 89, 95, 100 right, 105, 107, 108 top, 123 top, 126 right, 140 right, 164 left, 165 top

Mary Gore: pages 26, 35 bottom, 85 top right

Mark Turner: pages 35 top, 51 bottom, 91, 92, 106, 123 bottom, 136, 137, 146, 158 bottom, 173, 181, 198, 208 right

Martin Walsh: page 154 right

Peter Erskine: page 143 top right

Richie Steffens: pages 93, 94, 127, 142, 165 bottom, 194

Sue White: page 102

All other photographs by the author.

Index

Plant Directory entries appear in **bold type.**

About the author

After obtaining an honours degree in horticulture from London University, Keith Wiley spent twenty-five years as head gardener at the Garden House in Devon. There he evolved a gardening style based on modifying natural landscapes from around the globe. The garden he created there was described by national commentators as "one of the most exciting and innovative gardens in Britain today" and the best example of "leading-edge horticulture" in the United Kingdom.

© FIONA GILSENAN

Keith is a regular contributor to horticultural and lifestyle magazines, and has appeared on many gardening television programmes in the United Kingdom. Over the last ten years, Keith and his wife, Ros, have created a new garden from a bare field at Wildside, where they run their own nursery. Keith is the author of two other gardening books and has lectured widely all over the world.